Counter-Radicalization Bot Research

Using Social Bots to Fight Violent Extremism

WILLIAM MARCELLINO, MADELINE MAGNUSON, ANNE STICKELLS,
BENJAMIN BOUDREAUX, TODD C. HELMUS, EDWARD GEIST,
ZEV WINKELMAN

Prepared for the Department of State and the Combating Terrorism Technical Support Office
Approved for public release; distribution unlimited

RAND NATIONAL DEFENSE RESEARCH INSTITUTE

For more information on this publication, visit www.rand.org/t/RR2705

Library of Congress Cataloging-in-Publication Data is available for this publication.
ISBN: 978-1-9774-0394-0

Published by the RAND Corporation, Santa Monica, Calif.

Cover: monsitj/Adobe Stock.

Preface

Given the success violent extremist groups have had online—recruiting, funding, and messaging—the U.S. government (USG) has an interest in effective, agile, and scalable online responses. This report examines the applicability of automated social media (SM) accounts, known as *bots*, to address this problem. While this report was primarily directed at countering groups like the Islamic State of Iraq and the Levant (ISIL), the findings are also applicable to the growing threat of adversary state-sponsored SM information operations. Readers will find an overview of bot technology, a discussion of legal and ethical considerations around bot deployment, a framework for assessing risk/reward in bot operations, and recommendations for the USG in developing and deploying such bot programs. The research reported here was completed in August 2018 and underwent security review with the sponsor and the Defense Office of Prepublication and Security Review before public release.

This research was sponsored by the U.S. Department of State and the Combating Terrorism Technical Support Office and conducted within the International Security and Defense Policy Center of the RAND National Security Research Division (NSRD), which operates the National Defense Research Institute (NDRI), a federally funded research and development center sponsored by the Office of the Secretary of Defense, the Joint Staff, the Unified Combatant Commands, the Navy, the Marine Corps, the defense agencies, and the defense intelligence enterprise.

For more information on the RAND International Security and Defense Policy Center, see www.rand.org/nsrd/ndri/centers/isdp or contact the director (contact information is provided on the webpage).

Contents

Figures and Tables

Figures

Tables

Summary

The speed and diffusion of online recruitment for violent extremist organizations (VEOs) such as the Islamic State of Iraq and the Levant (ISIL) have challenged existing efforts to effectively intervene and engage in counter-radicalization in the digital space. This problem contributes to global instability and violence. Groups like ISIL identify susceptible individuals through open social media (SM) dialogue and eventually seek private conversations online and offline for recruiting. This shift from open and discoverable online dialogue to private and discreet recruitment can happen quickly and offers a short window for intervention before the conversation and the targeted individuals disappear.

The counter-radicalization messaging enterprise of the U.S. government (USG) may benefit from a sophisticated capability to rapidly detect targets of VEO recruitment efforts and deliver counter-radicalization content to them. Our report examines the applicability of promising emerging technology tools, particularly automated SM accounts known as bots, to this problem. While this report was initially narrowly conceived as a response to ISIL-like groups, our findings have broader applicability; the report has implications for any attempt to counter the growing threat of state-sponsored propagandists conducting disinformation campaigns or radicalizing U.S. domestic extremists online. While technology in this area is rapidly advancing, we hope the insights and recommendations in this report will still be valuable even as specifics change.

In the following pages, we assess the feasibility and advisability of the USG employing social bot technology for counter-radicalization and related purposes. Our analysis draws on interviews[1] with a range of subject-matter experts (SMEs) from industry, government, and academia, as well as reviews of legal and ethical considerations of using bots; the literature on the development and application of bot technology; and case studies on past uses of social bots to influence individuals, gather information, and conduct messaging campaigns. For readers newer to bot technology, Table S.1 defines basic relevant terms.

Table S.1
Bot Terminology

Term	Definition
Bot	Interactive software deployed on SM to replace or augment human efforts across a range of purposes and thus requiring some kind of artificial intelligence (AI), sociality, and linguistic capability.
Botmaster	Person or group controlling a network of bots for coordinated action.
Sock puppet	SM entity (including bots) posing as a real-world person but is actually artificial and controlled by a distinct entity. A single operator may run multiple sock puppets.
Troll	SM entity dedicated to antisocial behavior. In this context, *troll* refers to organizational or state-controlled entities engaged in harmful information-related activities such as spreading propaganda.
Social media (SM) platform	SM technology and service provider (e.g., Twitter or Facebook).
Application programming interface (API)	Tool set and rules for building software applications (e.g., bots).
Artificial intelligence (AI)	Machine-based intelligence; in this context, it ranges from simple conversation rules to sophisticated algorithms mimicking human behavior.

[1] RAND's Human Subjects Protection Committee determined that our research did not constitute generalizable research and was exempt from review.

Bot Types

Bots are used in a wide variety of ways, resulting in a range of intended and incidental impacts. Table S.2 lists the different types of bots examined in this chapter as well as briefly describing their intended purposes. Each bot type, along with associated use cases, is surveyed further in the following section.

Table S.2
Bot Types

Name	Description
Influence bots	Bots that engage with users to influence them in a certain direction, frequently by providing them with information that promotes the cause the bot is designed to support.
Astroturf bots	Bots that inflate the statistics or trendiness of a message or user by tweeting, liking, and following within a circle of amplifier bots.
Noise bots	Bots that disrupt communication and information being spread by an opposition group by diluting opposing content.
Smokescreen bots	Bots that try to disrupt a user's action or purpose by misdirecting or distracting an audience from their initial interest using alternative news or information.
Disinformation bots	Bots that widely spread false information, leading to false narratives.
Matchmaker bots	Bots that increase cooperation and information among users by connecting individuals who share similar interests but have not engaged with each other.
Harassment bots	Bots that harass users, forcing them out of a social space.
Harvest bots	Bots that engage or friend people to gain access to sensitive information.
Masquerade bots	Bots that pretend to be human in an attempt to keep a target user from engaging with actual humans instead.

Findings

Lessons from Current Bot Technology and Implementation

Our case studies, conducted in 2017, showcase bots empowering humans in scalable ways but also identify some constraints to the operational success of bots, which can often be outmaneuvered by human opponents. Lessons learned relate to the importance of tailoring bots to specific environments. These contextual factors include the platforms, cultures, and governmental regimes in which a bot is deployed; the social bot's profile characteristics, such as apparent social influence and group identity; and the network characteristics of users that a bot is attempting to befriend or influence, such as friend counts and network density.

These tactical lessons can help maximize the success of a bot operation, but a bot network can only perform as well as its underlying technology. To that end, we assess bot technology in terms of a maturity model that divides bot functions into the categories of sensing, deciding, and acting. We assess that the field is somewhere in the middle of its development life cycle; bot technology has advanced enough to be substantially useful on SM but has a long way to go before realizing all of its potential for both use and abuse. For instance, the next generation of bots likely will move beyond text generation to audio and video manipulation.

Legal and Ethical Issues Raised by Bot Programs

USG deployment of bots raises concerns touching on free speech, the Establishment Clause, privacy, the Smith-Mundt Act, international norms in cyberspace, and prohibitions on material support to terrorist groups.[2] The technology industry will be affected by trade-offs struck between the efficacy and transparency of certain bot programs, particularly as many SM platforms' terms of service (ToS) restrict bot behavior.

---

[2] The particular concern here is how courts might interpret plausibly effective interventions against extremism. For example, could a bot intervention meant to help at-risk populations access counseling be interpreted by courts as violating prohibitions on providing material support to terrorists?

In assessing the legal and ethical risks of bot programs, details matter; risks vary by bot type, target, deployer, and objective. This understanding informs the following conclusions:

1. Bot programs, even if used exclusively domestically, have international consequences, potentially setting precedents that normalize other states' actions. Bots that interfere with the confidentiality, integrity, or availability of information might be seen as actions that threaten cybersecurity.
2. The USG must integrate information it collects via bots into established mechanisms for collecting information and protecting privacy. Firewalls with law enforcement or international partners may benefit any bot programs that focus on counter-radicalization rather than counterterrorism (CT).
3. The USG should not use a bot to conduct actions that would be legally or ethically prohibited if done without the bot but maintaining honesty and transparency will alleviate some ethical risk. Having bots assume false identities in "human" disguises will tend to heighten legal and ethical concerns. Any promotion of false information will raise serious legal and ethical flags. Publicly articulating general principles for how the USG will deploy bots may bolster transparency while protecting sensitive operational details.
4. Partnering with internet platforms will further mitigate some risks. Determining whether bots comply with the ToS of internet and SM platforms will be necessary for any bot program. Any perception that the USG is pressuring or coercing internet platforms via bots to remove protected content will also likely raise red flags. However, seeking permission of internet platforms before the deployment of bots may help avoid strain with SM platforms.

Assessment of Bot Concepts of Operation for Risks and Opportunities

We propose a detailed framework for assessing the key components and variables of a bot program for strengths, weaknesses, risks, and opportunities; these criteria should then be applied to 12 notional types of bot programs to articulate a method for assessing bot concepts of operations. In Tables S.3–S.5, green indicates relatively few limitations/concerns and thus relative confidence, yellow indicates consider-

Table S.3
Concepts of Action: Influence and Inform

Option	Description	Technical Feasibility	General User Risks	Builder Risks	Potential Impact
Matchmaker	Connect support and at-risk communities				
Influence	Engage at-risk accounts one-on-one				
Prompter	Internal-facing bot auto-suggests responses				
Dis/Inform	Broadcast beneficial messages				
Astroturf	Amplify exposure of anti-extremist content				

Table S.4
Concepts of Action: Degrade/Disrupt Violent Extremist Networks

Option	Description	Technical Feasibility	General User Risks	Builder Risks	Potential Impact
Noise	Hijack extremist hashtags with unrelated spam				
Policeman	Detect and flag extremist accounts for takedown				
Exposer	"Out" other bot or troll accounts as bots or trolls				
Zombie	Take over opposing bot network				
Masquerade	Serve as false targets for extremist recruiters				

Table S.5
Concepts of Action: Collect Intelligence

Option	Description	Technical Feasibility	General User Risks	Builder Risks	Potential Impact
Harvest	Lure extremist engagement to collect personally identifiable information (PII)				
Mousetrap	Serve as false recruitment target to gain access to closed VE networks				

able limitations/concerns and thus caution, and orange indicates serious limitations/concerns and thus high caution.

Any definitive determination of risk and opportunity ultimately depends on the details of a proposed bot operation. However, a few relative judgments about the promise of these general concepts of action can be made.

1. In the category of bots that seeks to influence target audiences, the most feasible bots in terms of available technology and risk appear to be matchmaker bots, which connect at-risk individuals with support communities; and prompter bots, which autosuggest responses on an internal-facing interface.
2. Among bots that attempt to degrade or disrupt violent extremist (VE) networks, an exposer bot that transparently "outs" sock puppet accounts as bots or trolls seems to be the most immediately practicable, combining technical feasibility with relatively low risk for both the builder and general populations of SM users.
3. For bots that collect intelligence, harvest bots—which target friend accounts to gain access to their private profile information—are more technologically feasible than mousetrap bots, which seek to gain access to closed VE networks.

While rapidly developing bot technology shows great promise for use in counter-radicalization campaigns, any USG use of bots faces significant legal and ethical hazards. Bot program designers should attempt to maximize benefits by carefully tailoring bot programs along contextual factors while minimizing risks by maintaining as much honesty and transparency as possible. When weighing proposed bot programs, decisionmakers should carefully balance anticipated rewards against the many legal and ethical perils associated with automated intervention and messaging campaigns against VEOs like ISIL.

This review of bot technology and applications (through 2017) yielded two insights that in turn inform our recommendations.

1. The use of bots is a viable approach for a range of technologically feasible, plausibly effective interventions.
2. Because automated interventions can operate rapidly without human oversight, there is increased risk of unexpected negative outcomes. Decisionmakers must carefully weigh the risks and potential rewards of proposed automated bot programs.

Recommendations

U.S. agencies should keep the following practical and technical considerations in mind and weigh the following contextual factors when contemplating and designing bot programs.

1. Leverage commercial development of bot technology, as industry investment in this rapidly evolving space has yielded significant progress.
2. Tailor bots to the environment in which they are to be deployed, such as platform structures of engagement or the culture of government censorship among the target audience; this will maximize credibility in sensitive contexts and help avoid disasters resulting from unanticipated mismatches.
3. Carefully craft the profile characteristics of proposed bots, as in-group avatars with high follower counts are more likely to attract positive engagement.
4. Pay attention to the network characteristics of users the bot is seeking to engage, such as friend counts of individual target

users or whether target users are connected merely by topic of interest or preexist as a dense network of social connection; skeptical users are more likely to engage with accounts with whom they are already connected by social friends.

U.S. agencies should consider the following suggestions on how to mitigate the legal and ethical risks of any proposed bot program.

1. In light of the USG's leading role in the still rapidly evolving world of cyberspace, analyze the international precedent that may be set by any proposed bot program to avoid normalizing other states' invasive actions and behaviors that erode cybersecurity by interfering with the confidentiality, integrity, or availability of information online.
2. In response to concerns about the Establishment Clause, free speech, privacy, and the Smith-Mundt Act, focus engagement on narrowly targeted audiences of concern abroad; avoid targeting users based on religious criteria; and where deemed appropriate, erect firewalls between certain bot programs and law enforcement, intelligence agencies, or international partners.
3. With respect to SM platform's ToS and possible issues, seek companies' permission before deploying bots whenever necessary and practicable.
4. Given the likelihood of U.S.-sponsored bot activities becoming public knowledge, make USG bot operations as transparent as possible, within operational constraints. This will help mitigate backlash and associated negative consequences.
5. To ensure legal compliance, we recommend specific legal review for each bot deployment operation, under the applicable titles.

The USG should consider undertaking the following action items:

1. Communicate across agency lines about bot technology initiatives to develop a common conceptual framework and cross-agency operating picture.
2. Conduct a full interagency legal review regarding principles that USG bot programs should follow.

3. Promulgate doctrine about how USG actors intend to conduct operations to maximize transparency even while protecting sensitive operational details.
4. Test the efficacy and advisability of bot programs gradually by collaborating with nongovernmental organizations (NGOs) or partner nations or by implementing an internal-facing bot program.
5. Promote bot-detection technologies to make it harder for adversaries to engage in bot-enabled deception.

Acknowledgments

Many individuals contributed to the completion of this report. We are particularly grateful to the many subject-matter experts who generously agreed to be interviewed on behalf of this project. We also want to thank Drew Lomax, program manager, Irregular Warfare & Evolving Threats (Combating Terrorism Technical Support Office [CTTSO]), Department of Defense (DoD); and Brian Lewis, deputy director, Technical Programs (Bureau of Counter Terrorism), Department of State (DoS), for their support and guidance. Without them, this project would never have happened. We are also grateful for the oversight and coordination provided by Vanessa Lee Jones, program analyst, Irregular Warfare & Evolving Threats (CTTSO), DoD; and for the technical expertise and involvement of Brian Fairlie, senior data scientist, Office of Analysis, Science, and Technology (Global Engagement Center), DoS.

Abbreviations

ACLU	American Civil Liberties Union
AI	artificial intelligence
API	application programming interface
CONOP	concept of operation
CT	counterterrorism
CVE	counter violent extremism
DL	deep learning
DoD	U.S. Department of Defense
GEC	Global Engagement Center
IC	intelligence community
IO	information operations
ISIL	Islamic State of Iraq and the Levant, also known as the Islamic State
ML	machine learning
NGO	nongovernmental organization
NLG	natural language generation
NLU	natural language understanding
PII	personally identifiable information
REST	representational state transfer
SM	social media
SME	subject-matter expert

ToS	terms of service
UK	United Kingdom
USG	United States government
VE	violent extremist
VEO	violent extremist organization

CHAPTER ONE

Social Chatbots: An Introduction

The proliferation of social networking sites in the past decade has revolutionized the way people around the world consume news and formulate opinions and is becoming a central battlefield for communication networks and information environments. Meanwhile, emerging technologies powered by data analytics, artificial intelligence (AI), and machine learning (ML) are enabling the scalable application of algorithmic solutions to new problems; this includes the creation and development of automated social media (SM) accounts, referred to as social bots.

This convergence of trends represents an opportunity for the United States and its allies as well as a significant threat from adversaries. Russia has proven adept at blending online networks of social bots and trolls to influence information environments while recruitment apparatuses of the Islamic State of Iraq and the Levant (ISIL) have exploited automated SM accounts to disseminate propaganda. At the same time, technology companies are actively exploring ways to use social bots to interact with people in positive ways, from providing timely practical assistance and medical advice to matchmaking at-risk users with emotional support networks.

This new wave of technological development raises critical and timely questions for the U.S. government (USG). What are possible applications of bot technology to this contested information space? What are the legal and ethical implications of these applications? How should the USG weigh the potential high rewards of implementing bot programs with the equally high risks of such an enterprise? Accordingly, this report attempts to orient USG actors to the opportunities and risks inherent in the application of social bot technology to the mission set of countering online radicalization. We recognize that not all bots are nefarious; in fact, as we detail later, some bots have real potential for positive impacts. However, we also recognize that potential adversaries are already using bots in nefarious ways, increasing the urgency around analyzing bot use in national security contexts.

The speed and diffusion of online recruitment for violent extremist organizations (VEOs) such as ISIL have outpaced existing technological counter-recruitment intervention, contributing to global instability and violence. Groups like ISIL identify susceptible individuals through open SM dialogue and eventually seek private conversations online and offline to recruit them. This shift from open and discoverable online dialogue to private and discreet recruiting can happen quickly and offers a short window for intervention before the conversation and the targeted individuals disappear.

The USG's counter-radicalization messaging enterprise lacks a sophisticated capability to rapidly deliver counter-radicalization content to ISIL's obscure radicalization targets. Our report researched the applicability of promising new technology tools, especially automated SM accounts (bots), to this problem.

In the following chapters, to help research and evaluate any potential use of bots by the USG in counter-radicalization messaging, we first assess the state of bot technology through 2017 and its projected evolution. We then review legal and ethical considerations, articulate and assess models for detecting and responding to online radicalization, and evaluate the risks and opportunities of using bots in online countermessaging. Finally, drawing on this research, we articulate specific recommendations for how the USG can most effectively integrate bot technology into existing engagement efforts against VEOs.

Many of the observations and insights in the following chapters came from the 18 interviews we conducted with 22 subject-matter experts (SMEs). The interviewees came from a number of relevant fields, including technology, law, and counter violent extremism (CVE). We interviewed four academic experts with histories of government or collaboration in the fields of technology, cyberspace, or extremism; two directors of an online CVE outreach program; three legal scholars focused on cybersecurity and digital threats to civil society; three federal government officials working on CVE and strategic communications issues; and ten industry experts ranging from representatives of SM platforms to designers of bot programs.

In the rest of this chapter, we present a short introduction to bots. We then provide a three-part overview of bot technology through 2017, primarily as informed by the academic literature.

1. A review of the mechanics of implementing bots on SM platforms
2. A review of bot types and their purposes, including a typology of bots
3. A review of continuing technological challenges in bot development.

We then summarize our overview of bots as a launching point for a more detailed dive into illustrative case studies of bot use.

An Introduction to Bots

Facebook, Twitter, and additional social platforms have had significant impact since their appearance in the mid-2000s. Today, SM platforms have over one billion active users, and individuals' engagement continues to grow.[1] As these platforms have developed, their influence has increased in many areas, including politics, the economy, and society. This influence creates a fertile ground for both data gathering and manipulation, and social bots provide a means of achieving these goals.

Bots, a shortened term referring to software robots, started to develop when computers were first used. Early bots in the late 1980s and early 1990s served simple functions like gaming and managing chat rooms.[2] Today, bots are more complex and are frequently used

---

[1] Maeve Duggan et al., "Social Media Update 2014," *Pew Research Center*, January 9, 2015.

[2] Amit Kumar Tyagi and G. Aghila, "A Wide Scale Survey on Botnet," *International Journal of Computer Applications*, Vol. 34, No. 9, 2011.

in botnets, which refer to a collection of bots that are controlled by a single user, often referred to as a botmaster or botherder.[3] Bots are now used in a variety of ways, including spreading information and disinformation, connecting and disrupting social networks, and harvesting people's personal information.

Increasingly, politicians, militaries, government organizations, and other groups have used bots to manipulate public opinions and to disrupt natural discourse on social platforms.[4] For example, bots have been used for political purposes in a growing number of countries, including Argentina, Australia, Azerbaijan, Bahrain, China, Iran, Italy, Mexico, Morocco, Russia, South Korea, Saudi Arabia, Turkey, the United Kingdom (UK), the United States, and Venezuela.[5] Today, over 23 million active users on Twitter are social bots,[6] and in 2012 a Facebook report revealed that 5–6 percent of accounts are fake.[7]

Bot Technology Review

The following section presents the results of our technology review,[8] orienting the reader to the field of bot technology. We first explain implementation strategies for bots on SM platforms. We then present a typology of bot types, along with detailed explanations and illustrative examples of each type's use. The final section highlights ongoing research challenges relating to bots.

---

[3] Tyagi and Aghila, 2011.

[4] Samuel Woolley, "Automating Power: Social Bot Interference in Global Politics," *First Monday*, Vol. 21, No. 4, 2016.

[5] Woolley, 2016.

[6] Woolley, 2016.

[7] Norah Abokhodair, Daisy Yoo, and David McDonald, "Dissecting a Social Botnet: Growth, Content and Influence in Twitter," *Proceedings of the 18th ACM Conference on Computer Supported Cooperative Work & Social Computing*, New York: Association for Computing Machinery, March 2015.

[8] For more detail on the review method, please see Appendix A.

Implementing Bots on SM Platforms

The implementation strategies employed in making bots vary as much as the diverse applications of bot technology. Bots range from simple scripts of less than a page of code to baroque experiments showcasing the latest AI techniques. In practice, most bots tend toward the simpler end of this spectrum. As is often the case, when building a bot it is generally best to employ the simplest approach that provides good real-world results.

Platform Application Programming Interfaces

The ease of developing a bot that interacts with a particular SM platform such as Twitter or Facebook depends on the availability of an application programming interface (API) for that platform. While typically intended to facilitate the creation of apps that interact with SM platforms, APIs can greatly simplify the task of making bots because they spare the bot builder the task of developing an interface to that SM platform themselves.

Twitter and Facebook have ambiguous and constantly evolving policies on the subject of implementation affordances. However, both of these platforms have APIs that make building rudimentary bots easy enough for even a novice programmer, as libraries for popular programming languages (often developed by individuals outside of SM companies) interfacing with these platforms can be combined with other publicly available libraries for ML and pattern-matching.

For instance, Twitter provides both a representational state transfer (REST) API that can be used to write programs that post tweets and read author profiles and a streaming API that can be used to follow particular users and topics or conduct data mining.[9] Software libraries providing access to this API are available for a wide array of programming languages, allowing developers to use whatever language they find most suitable. Particularly popular languages such as Python have multiple libraries for interacting with the Twitter API.[10] Similarly, Face-

---

9 Twitter, "Twitter Developer Documentation," webpage, May 8, 2017.

10 Twitter, "Twitter Libraries," webpage, undated a.

book offers APIs for various aspects of its services, including one specifically for its Messenger platform, and libraries exist for a wide variety of programming languages to interact with them.[11] Microsoft, meanwhile, offers a preview version of its "Bot Framework," which aims to provide a unified API for bots interacting with a variety of services, including Skype, Slack, Facebook Messenger, Kik, and Office 365 email.[12]

Avoiding Detection

Many bots, particularly commercial bots, operate openly as bots. However, as of 2017, many of the types and uses of bots that are relevant to this report are for information operations (IO) and intelligence purposes and thus are usually disguised as human personae. Other bots intended to boost advertising campaigns and the visibility of commercial products also try to pass as human users. While different platforms have different rules, using bots surreptitiously generally violates platforms' terms of service (ToS). This has led to a kind of arms race between platforms and bot makers, as platforms try to detect and remove disguised bots while bot programmers and deployers try to evade detection.

The availability of APIs and libraries allows even a novice programmer to develop his or her own bots, but making bots evince sophisticated behavior or coordinating large botnets is considerably more challenging. Much of the difficulty of developing and maintaining bots eligible for platform suspension involves avoiding interdiction. Today, SM platforms make attempts to detect and shut down bot activities. For example, Facebook uses the Facebook Immune System, an adversarial learning system that performs checks on every read and write action that occurs on the platform, to detect and stop bots. However, programs like this are far from perfect, and a study by the University of British Columbia found that Facebook identified and suspended

---

[11] Facebook, "Documentation," Facebook for Developers, undated. For instance, the documentation for the Python library fbchat includes code for a simple Facebook Messenger echobot a mere dozen lines long. Python Software Foundation, "fbchat 0.9.0: Facebook Chat (Messenger) for Python," webpage, November 21, 2016.

[12] Microsoft, "Bot Framework FAQ," webpage, February 20, 2019.

only 20 percent of the study's bot accounts after other Facebook users flagged the accounts as suspicious.[13] This example shows the attempts of a platform to stop and shut down bot accounts as well as the limitations of a platform's ability to do so.

Even when bots are not caught, their impact can still be limited by platform operations and characteristics. In a case where 25,860 bots released content attempting to disrupt discussion of Russian parliamentary election results in 2011, the impact of "noisy" bots was limited by Twitter's relevance ranking of tweets. In "Top" view of search results, Twitter shows content based on relevance and popularity as opposed to "Latest" view, in which results are ranked purely by recency. In the case of Russia's parliamentary elections, Twitter's search relevance algorithm substantially reduced the impact of the bot account noise, eliminating 53 percent of the fraudulent tweets.[14] Similarly, influence bots used by Venezuelan politicians to boost retweets of certain content created an effect, but it was subtle: only 10 percent of retweets came from bots or bot platforms.[15] Many SM platforms, including Twitter, welcome benevolent or nonaggressive bots that do not pretend to be actual users.[16] "Honest" bots such as these can avoid the need to obfuscate bots' true nature and can potentially be much simpler as a result.[17]

However, the utility of many bots depends on their ability to pass as humans. For bots to avoid detection and suspension by SM platforms, bot makers employ certain tactics. Strategies to avoid negative

---

[13] Yazan Boshmaf et al., "The Socialbot Network: When Bots Socialize for Fame and Money," *Proceedings of the Twenty-Seventh Annual Computer Security Applications Conference*, New York: Association for Computing Machinery, 2011.

[14] Kurt Thomas, Chris Grier, and Vern Paxson, "Adapting Social Spam Infrastructure for Political Censorship," *Proceedings of the 5th USENIX Workshop on Large-Scale Exploits and Emergent Threats*, Berkeley, Calif.: USENIX Association, 2012.

[15] Michelle Forelle et al., *Political Bots and the Manipulation of Public Opinion in Venezuela*, July 25, 2015.

[16] Emilio Ferrara et al., "The Rise of Social Bots," *Communications of the ACM*, Vol. 59, No. 7, 2016, pp. 96–104.

[17] Clayton Davis et al., "BotOrNot: A System to Evaluate Social Bots," *Proceedings of the 25th International Conference Companion on World Wide Web*, New York: Association for Computing Machinery, February 2, 2016.

attention necessarily depend on the bot-detection techniques and user policies of the SM platform in question, both of which are constantly evolving. Authorities have varying opinions on which techniques to detect SM bots are most promising.[18] Since the business models of most SM firms depend on monetizing user data, accounts associated with bots threaten their bottom line. Bots often attempt to avoid automated systems that block or delete such accounts by trying to mimic human behavior in order to spoof them.

Both individual bots and botnets can employ a range of means to evade detection. Many of these techniques were developed and employed as part of the Twitter Bot Challenge, a competition of the Defense Advanced Research Projects Agency in which teams raced to identify a known group of pro-vaccination influence bots on Twitter.[19]

Many bot-detection tools employ ML models to ascertain the activity patterns of human users and flag possible bot accounts that deviate from these norms. To evade such techniques, some bots attempt to hide their true nature by carrying out relatively "human" tasks much or most of the time. This in turn leads to an "arms race" between bot detectors and bots as each side tries to keep one step ahead of the other.

A related means of detecting bots involves account age. Recently created accounts stick out more obviously as bot or spam accounts. Therefore, "aging" bot accounts by creating them long before they are used in a conspicuous messaging campaign and by gradually building up histories of varied posts helps evade detection.[20] Bot accounts can also be purchased prefabricated and already aged from various websites, using credit cards or anonymous digital currency.[21]

---

[18] See Davis et al., 2016; and Jinxue Zhang, Rui Zhang, Yanchao Zhang, and Guanhua Yan, "The Rise of Social Botnets: Attacks and Countermeasures," Cornell University arXiv:1603.02714 [cs.SI], March 8, 2016.

[19] V. S. Subrahmanian et al., "The DARPA Twitter Bot Challenge," *Computer*, Vol. 49, No. 6, June 2016.

[20] Interview with government expert working on CVE and online radicalization, December 9, 2016; interview with tech industry expert who liaises with USG clients and previously worked at DoD, December 15, 2016.

[21] For one such site, see BuyAccs.com (undated), which advertises bulk email and SM accounts.

Other bot-detection tools identify bots by examining users' social graphs. Rudimentary bots will often have no friends or followers while even more sophisticated ones will have a social network considerably different from that of a typical human user. Sophisticated bot builders sometimes construct botnets specifically to work around this type of bot-detection technique. By designing their bots to interact with each other in a way at least somewhat resembling human accounts, they can provide cover for their activities.[22]

One of the last lines of defense used by SM platforms against bots involves user reporting. Bots that provoke SM users into flagging bot accounts for ToS violations will suffer a high rate of suspension. One interviewee suggested hard-coding rules for simplistic bots such as "never respond to one person with same tweet twice, and disengage after two messages," reasoning that "the annoyance threshold generally has to be higher than just two unwanted tweets for people to report it."[23] This also relates to bot-detection methods that rely on anomalies in scale; minimizing the scale or volume of bot activity will minimize the risk of account suspension and removal.[24]

Implementation Complexity

Available discussions of bot implementation techniques predominantly focus on the simpler types of bots. Although few authors address the question directly, there appears to be an implicit consensus that the overwhelming majority of the bots active today are based on relatively simple implementations, as there is no practical advantage to developing a more sophisticated implementation than is strictly necessary. Unfortunately, there appears to be no general survey of the relative use of different bot implementation techniques or of the implementers themselves. While swift progress in bot implementation tends to

---

22 Ferrara et al., 2016.

23 Interview with bot industry expert with intelligence community (IC) background, October 20, 2016.

24 Interview with government expert working on CVE and online radicalization, December 9, 2016; interview with tech industry expert who liaises with USG clients and previously worked at DoD, December 15, 2016.

outpace academic publishing, most observers concur that cutting-edge techniques are too immature for general deployment. Systems employing online learning and deep neural networks are difficult to build and maintain, and at present (through 2017) they do not provide advantages that compensate for this in most circumstances. Bots using such advanced techniques are usually research experiments rather than practical implementations.[25] In part, this results from the imperfect state of bot-detection techniques. Because of the huge number of bots and the intentional obfuscation of many of them, it is difficult to identify a representative sample to serve as the basis of such a study.

Bot Types

Bots are used in a wide variety of ways, resulting in a range of intended and incidental impacts. Table 1.1 lists the different types of bots examined in this chapter and briefly describes their intended purposes. Each bot type, along with associated use cases, is surveyed further in the following section.

Influence Bots

Influence bots, or bots that engage with users to influence them in a certain direction, are a common type of SM bot. Influence bots will often attempt to influence users by providing them with information that promotes the cause the bot is designed to support. The term *influence bot* is used consistently to describe this type of bot. Influence bots can have an impact, as Chad Edwards and his team found in their 2014 study on communication credibility. The study was composed of 240 undergraduate students, who used established source credibility metrics to rate a mock Centers for Disease Control and Preven-

---

[25] For examples, see Alan Ritter, Colin Cherry, and William Dolan, "Data-Driven Response Generation in Social Media," *Proceedings of the Conference on Empirical Methods in Natural Language Processing*, Stroudsburg, Pa.: Association for Computational Linguistics, July 2011; and Alessandro Sordoni et al., "A Neural Network Approach to Context-Sensitive Generation of Conversational Responses," *Proceedings of the North American Chapter of the Association for Computational Linguistics: Human Language Technologies*, Denver, Colo., June 22, 2015.

Table 1.1
Bot Types

Name	Description
Influence bots	Bots that engage with users to influence them in a certain direction, frequently by providing them with information that promotes the cause the bot is designed to support.
Astroturf bots	Bots that inflate the statistics or trendiness of a message or user by tweeting, liking, and following within a circle of amplifier bots.
Noise bots	Bots that disrupt communication and information being spread by an opposition by diluting opposing content.
Smokescreen bots	Bots that try to disrupt a user's action or purpose by misdirecting or distracting an audience from their initial interest using alternative news or information.
Disinformation bots	Bots that spread false information widely, leading to false narratives.
Matchmaker bots	Bots that increase cooperation and information among users by connecting individuals who share similar interests but have not engaged with each other.
Harassment bots	Bots that harass users, forcing them out of a social space.
Harvest bots	Bots that engage or friend people to gain access to sensitive information.
Masquerade bots	Bots that pretend to be human in an attempt to keep a target user from engaging with actual humans instead.

tion (CDC) Twitter page. Half of the participants viewed a version of the page with the author listed as "CDC Bot" while the other half saw the same ten tweets as coming from "CDC Scientist." Ultimately, the study found users did not notice significant differences in perception of credibility, communication, and intent to interact between the self-proclaimed bot and human. The authors claimed the study demonstrated "that Twitterbots can be viewed as credible, attractive, competent in communication, and interactional."[26] Even bots that appear

[26] Chad Edwards et al., "Is That a Robot Running the Social Media Feed? Testing the Differences in Perceptions of Communication Quality for a Human Agent and a Bot Agent on Twitter," *Computers in Human Behavior*, Vol. 33, April 2014.

untrustworthy—by not announcing that they are bots while engaging only in simple, repetitive spamming—can be successful in this arena, according to experiments conducted by academics from the University of Turin. These researchers found "that an untrustworthy individual [a bot] can become very relevant and influential through very simple automated activity."[27] A group of researchers from the Federal University of Minas Gerais in Brazil created 120 fully automated social bots on Twitter, attracting 5,000 follows from almost 2,000 distinct users and receiving over 2,000 likes, retweets, or mentions. Impressively, over 20 percent of the bots earned Klout influence scores higher than 35 and amassed over 100 followers.[28]

Given these notable abilities, it is not surprising that there are a number of influence bots today. For example, pro-vaccine groups have employed influence bots to counter misinformation spread by anti-vaccine Twitter activists.[29] While this example demonstrates how these bots can be used to promote a social cause, politicians have frequently used these bots for personal gain. For instance, the Venezuelan government has used influence bots to spread its messages and counter political opposition.[30] Similarly, in a recent Mexican election, the Institutional Revolutionary Party used thousands of bots to promote its message and help it land messages on Twitter's trending topics feed.[31] Russia also operates influence bots, using "Kremlin bots" to troll opposition and regularly promote pro-Putin hashtags.[32]

---

[27] Luca Maria Aiello et al., "People Are Strange When You're a Stranger: Impact and Influence of Bots on Social Networks," *Proceedings of the Sixth International AAAI Conference on Weblogs and Social Media*, Menlo Park, Calif.: Association for the Advancement of Artificial Intelligence, 2012.

[28] Carlos Freitas et al., "Reverse Engineering Socialbot Infiltration Strategies in Twitter," Cornell University arXiv:1405.4927 [cs.SI], May 20, 2014.

[29] Subrahmanian et al., 2016.

[30] Forelle et al., 2015.

[31] Mike Orcutt, "Twitter Mischief Plagues Mexico's Election," *MIT Technology Review*, June 21, 2012.

[32] Yazan Boshmaf et al., "Design and Analysis of a Social Botnet," *Computer Networks: The International Journal of Computer and Telecommunications Networking*, Vol. 2, No. 57, February 2013, pp. 556–578.

One final example of influence bots manifested during the Brexit debate when researchers from Oxford University and Corvinus University found that "the two single most active accounts on either side of the debate [were] bots."[33] Neither of these bots generated new content but instead retweeted messages from their side of the debate, repeating content that supported their message and collecting it in one place on their feed.

Astroturf Bots

Astroturf bots are another frequently employed type of bot that is used in a network to imitate grassroots activity or support for an idea or person. They often inflate the statistics or trendiness of a message or user by tweeting, liking, and following within a circle of amplifier bots. The term appeared in an article by Ratkiewicz[34] and has since been adopted by other sources. These actions can lend to a candidate or cause the appearance of support and importance as they create "the illusion of grassroots support for political aims."[35] Astroturf bots can improve a message or candidate's reputation since rumors gain traction and credibility as they are spread.[36]

Politicians commonly employ astroturf bots, and using these bots to increase a user's followers has become a political strategy worldwide.[37] For example, the Cuban dissident Yusnaby Perez reported that Venezuelan president Maduro had over 2,500 bots retweeting his messages.[38] During the 2013 Australian federal election, all four of the most popu-

---

[33] Philip Howard and Bence Kollanyi, "Bots, #StrongerIn, and #Brexit: Computational Propaganda During the UK-EU Referendum," Cornell University arXiv:1606.06356 [cs.SI], June 20, 2016.

[34] Jacob Ratkiewicz et al., "Truthy: Mapping the Spread of Astroturf in Microblog Streams," *Proceedings of the 20th International Conference Companion on World Wide Web*, New York: Association for Computing Machinery, 2011.

[35] David Cook et al., "Twitter Deception and Influence: Issues of Identity, Slacktivism, and Puppetry," *Journal of Information Warfare*, Vol. 13, No. 1, 2014.

[36] Davis et al., 2016.

[37] Forelle et al., 2015.

[38] Forelle et al., 2015.

lar politicians had significant numbers of fake followers. Of the most recent 50,000 followers for each of these candidates (including the incumbent prime minister and the leader of the opposition), roughly 40 percent came from fake accounts.[39] Politicians in the United States have also used this type of bot to boost their credibility and profile. For example, in 2012 Mitt Romney's Twitter account, which had been gaining an average of between 2,000 and 5,000 new users a day, gained 141,000 followers over a two-day period. Romney denied buying the followers, and while this is possible, it is clear that these new followers were bots.[40] During the most recent U.S. election, astroturf bots were also used during the presidential debates. During the first presidential debate, roughly one-third of pro-Trump Twitter traffic was driven by bots, compared with one-fifth of pro-Clinton traffic.[41] Similarly, in the second debate, one-third of pro-Trump Twitter traffic was driven by bots, while one-fourth of pro-Clinton traffic was driven by bots.[42] The researchers who discovered this suggested that these astroturf bots had a "modest but strategic role in the U.S. Presidential debates."[43]

Noise Bots

The job of a noise bot is to disrupt communication and information being spread by an opposition group and is accomplished by diluting opposing content. This is often done by overwhelming a hashtag with spam. While this technique does create "noise," other terms are also used to describe this type of bot, including *spam bot*. One example of another type of noise bot is a Google or Twitter bomb, in which web spam forces a search engine to give high relevancy to results that would

---

[39] Craig Butt and Thomas Hounslow, "Spambots Target Tweeting Pollies," *Sydney Morning Herald*, April 28, 2013.

[40] Alexander Furnas and Devin Gaffney, "Statistical Probability That Mitt Romney's New Twitter Followers Are Just Normal Users: 0%," *Atlantic*, July 31, 2012.

[41] Bence Kollanyi, Philip Howard, and Samuel Woolley, "Bots and Automation over Twitter During the First U.S. Presidential Debate," Data Memo 2016.2, Oxford, UK: Project on Computational Propaganda, 2016.

[42] Kollanyi, Howard, and Woolley, 2016.

[43] Kollanyi, Howard, and Woolley, 2016.

otherwise be unrelated. For example, in 2004 a Google bomb associated John Kerry with waffles.[44]

This type of bot has been used in a number of situations, many of them political. For example, in the 2011 Russian election an attacker used over 25,000 fraudulent Twitter accounts to send 440,793 tweets in an attempt to disrupt political conversations following the parliamentary election results.[45] The Mexican government has also used noise bots to disrupt and stifle public dissent by using spam tactics.[46]

Smokescreen Bots

Smokescreen bots are similar to noise bots in that they attempt to disrupt a user's action or purpose. Another common term used to describe these bots is *decoy bots*. However, *decoy bot* has also been used to describe other bot types, and so to avoid confusion in this review, this term was not used. Unlike noise bots, smokescreen bots use alternative news or information to try to misdirect or distract an audience from their initial interest. Abokhodair and her team discovered a smokescreen bot when they found what they termed "the Syrian social botnet" while researching the growth of a social botnet over time. The goal of this botnet was to divert attention from the Syrian civil war, and these bots achieved this purpose by releasing large amounts of content that was unrelated to the conflict while using hashtags frequently used to tag information related to the civil war. The content was often related to other foreign news or humanitarian crises.[47]

Disinformation

Disinformation bots are bots that spread false information widely, leading to false narratives, or that manipulate public opinion. These bots are frequently meant to cause social disruption or panic. Academic literature about bots includes examples of disinformation bot opera-

[44] Panagiotis Metaxas and Eni Mustafaraj, "Social Media and the Elections," *Science*, Vol. 338, October 26, 2012.

[45] Thomas, Grier, and Paxson, 2012.

[46] Woolley, 2016.

[47] Abokhodair, Yoo, and McDonald, 2015.

tions but does not use this term to distinguish disinformation bots from other bot types as they may overlap substantially with influence, astroturf, or smokescreen bots in terms of tactics but differ in intent and overall communication strategy.

Russia frequently uses disinformation bots, in the near and far abroad, such as when the country employed bots and trolls in an attempt to influence the 2016 presidential election by sowing confusion and spreading particular narratives.[48] In one particular example, the Putin administration used fake accounts to spread false rumors of atrocities performed by Ukrainian extremists. In one case, a profile of a supposed doctor shared a story of a tragedy in the city of Odessa. According to the narrative, Ukrainian extremists beat their victims before burning them alive, and the narrator was prevented from helping those he could save. However, research showed that the doctor's photo came from an advertising brochure, and the doctor did not exist.[49] In this case, it is likely that there was a human actor behind this sock puppet account, most likely a real person employed by a Russian troll farm.[50] However, these actions could be replicated with automated accounts, making this type of activity ripe for exploitation by bot networks.

Matchmaker Bots

Matchmaker bots increase cooperation and information among users by connecting individuals who share similar interests but have not engaged with each other. This type of bot did not have a set name in

---

[48] Clint Watts, "Disinformation: A Primer in Russian Active Measures and Influence Campaigns," statement prepared for a U.S. Senate Select Committee on Intelligence, Washington, D.C., March 30, 2017; Samuel Woolley and Douglas Guilbeault, *Computational Propaganda in the United States of America: Manufacturing Consensus Online*, Oxford, UK: University of Oxford, Working Paper No. 2017.5, May 2017.

[49] Paul Roderick Gregory, "Inside Putin's Campaign of Social Media Trolling and Faked Ukrainian Crimes," *Forbes*, May 11, 2014.

[50] Russian troll farms are entities that employ individuals to create and maintain fake SM accounts. These accounts are then used to spread false narratives, which have included an Ebola outbreak in Atlanta, a chemical hazard in Louisiana, and a rumor of an unarmed black woman being shot to death by police. Adrian Chen, "The Agency," *New York Times Magazine*, June 2, 2015.

the academic literature, and so the term *matchmaker bot* was coined for this report. As one example of a matchmaker bot, the lajello bot ran on a site for book lovers called aNobii.com, gathering information on users and then attempting to persuade users to add a new neighbor to their contact lists. The experiment found that "among the 361 users who created a social connection in the 36 hours after the recommendation . . . 52% followed the suggestion given by the bot."[51] While matchmaker bots do not appear to have been used widely at this point, it seems plausible that they may be used more extensively in the future. One envisioned application of a matchmaker bot involves banks, in which a user could be matched with their bank by a bot, and then the bot uses the match to communicate with the bank and make sure the user maintains their personal budget. Certain companies are already beginning to consider this potential.[52]

Harassment Bots

Harassment bots heckle or threaten target users, forcing them out of a public space. The intent of this type of bot is often to silence users online, as the harassment bots drive them away from their chosen platform of discourse. Russia has been known to employ this tactic, using accounts that look like real people to perform organized harassment, sometimes including threats of violence. Specifically, Russia uses these types of bots to silence political discourse, as harassment bots "discredit or silence people who wield influence in targeted realms, such as foreign policy or the Syrian civil war."[53]

Harvest Bots

Harvest bots are unlike other bots that have been discussed so far, as they do not work to spread information. Instead, they attempt to gather information on their targets. The term *harvest bot* is not used

---

[51] Aiello et al., 2012.

[52] Mary Wisniewski, "How Bots Can Connect Banks and Millennials," *American Banker*, August 1, 2016.

[53] Andrew Weisburd, Clint Watts, and J. M. Berger, "Trolling for Trump: How Russia Is Trying to Destroy Our Democracy," *War on the Rocks*, November 6, 2016.

in the literature, but as personal data have been "harvested" by bots, this term was used to categorize this type of bot in this review. Specifically, harvest bots engage or friend people to gain access to their personal information. While a user does have to engage with the bot in order for it to achieve this purpose, research has shown that people accept bot requests frequently. In one experiment, bots attained up to an 80-percent acceptance rate when they shared a mutual friend with the user.[54] One study conducted by Elyashar focused on this phenomenon and targeted employees of technology organizations; they assumed that these individuals would be more cognizant of bots and their potential impacts. Despite this, bots were still able to achieve acceptance rates of 50–70 percent from these employees.[55]

Masquerade Bots

Masquerade bots pretend to be human while communicating with users, with the intention of distracting users or taking up time that could otherwise be used to speak with actual people. These bots get users to waste their time trying to persuade bots instead of effectively using their time persuading humans. Because this type of bot acts like a human and masks its true nature, the term *masquerade bot* was chosen as a descriptor for this report. One instance of a masquerade bot found in the literature showcased the work of Nora Reed. Reed built several bots that acted like humans, posting "vaguely liberal" tweets such as "feminism is good" and then returning a canned response like "your [sic] wrong" and "Google it" when people replied. The bots, while not sophisticated, managed to get many people to argue with them.[56]

---

[54] Boshmaf et al., 2013.

[55] Aviad Elyashar et al., "Homing Socialbots: Intrusion on a Specific Organization's Employee Using Socialbots," *Proceedings of the 2013 IEEE/ACM International Conference on Advances in Social Networks Analysis and Mining*, New York: Association for Computing Machinery, August 2013.

[56] Caitlin Dewey, "This Bot Expertly Baits Internet Imbeciles into Losing Arguments," *Washington Post*, October 5, 2016.

Continuing Challenges

Unfortunately, at least through 2017, bots are generally better fitted for disrupting discourse in cyberspace than making a positive contribution to it. While exceptions exist, they remain rare compared with bots that aim to sell goods, steal personal information, or spread propaganda.[57] In large part, this is because large-scale constructive engagement with humans is difficult and strains state-of-the-art techniques. Progress in AI, however, might allow the creation of much more sophisticated bots with more potential to contribute to the social good.

Discourse Identification

To combat adversary discourse in cyberspace, bots need to be able to identify that discourse with a high degree of confidence. This remains the case whether they aim to engage humans in conversation or accomplish the much easier goal of disrupting adversary messaging. Further, they need to attain this capability in exchange for a reasonable investment of training data and developer time. Unfortunately, while ML techniques can likely enable discourse identification even in nontext media, they cannot do so as of 2017 without far more data and developer effort than are likely to be available in a time-critical policy context. Emerging AI techniques offer some promise for surmounting these obstacles, but they remain too immature to predict their ultimate success.

---

[57] One study found that Twitter bots presented as white users with a substantial number of followers could elicit a small but statistically significant reduction in the use of racial slurs by the humans they interacted with. Unfortunately, bots with fewer followers or presenting as African-American did not elicit a statistically significant response. Kevin Munger, "Tweetment Effects on the Tweeted: Experimentally Reducing Racist Harassment," *Political Behavior*, Vol. 39, No. 3, September 2017, pp. 629–649. Another project sought to use SM bots to crowdsource ideas from activists on how to combat corruption in Latin America. Saiph Savage, Andres Monroy-Hernandez, and Tobias Hollerer, "Botivist: Calling Volunteers to Action Using Online Bots," *Proceedings of the 19th ACM Conference on Computer-Supported Cooperative Work and Social Computing*, New York: Association for Computing Machinery, March 2016. A bot designed to correct users on Twitter who referred to Caitlin Jenner as "he" rather than "she" attracted considerable media attention, but its creator admitted that "reformees" whose minds had been changed by interacting with it were "very, very few." Caitlin Dewey, "I Created the Caitlyn Jenner Bot @she_not_he. This Is What I Learned," *Washington Post*, June 2, 2015.

Automated trolling is comparatively simple, but this is because trolls are both undiscriminating about their exact targets and unconcerned about collateral damage. For instance, implementing a bot that identified servers hosting online discourse containing a high proportion of mentions of a particular word or phrase and then launched an automated distributed denial of service attack against those servers would be trivially simple. But such an attack might disrupt misidentified legitimate discourse or cause economic losses to innocent people by interrupting other services on that network. Operating partially automated botnets with human oversight might alleviate the worst of these problems, but this could still run other risks, such as causing embarrassment for the United States if the botnets became public knowledge since disrupting discourse contradicts American values like freedom of expression. Bots capable of adaptive tactical countermessaging may therefore be more desirable, but to realize their promise they will need to combine features from two of the most challenging areas of AI research: natural language understanding (NLU) and automated planning and acting.

Natural Language Understanding and Generation

The aim of NLU is to make computers that "understand" language well enough to know what humans mean. While a tremendous amount of research has been done in this area over the past 60 years and has cultivated several distinct schools of thought on how to approach it, these systems still suffer from considerable shortcomings. The problem is that available NLU techniques all have trade-offs that make them difficult to apply to open-ended real-world tasks such as engaging in conversation with individuals on the internet. ML approaches exist that work well with training data, but they produce knowledge representations that do not readily allow for transfer learning—meaning they have to be retrained from scratch for each specific task.[58] Older "symbolic" approaches mapped discourse onto human-comprehensible

---

[58] Kyunghyun Cho, "Natural Language Understanding with Distributed Representation," lecture note for DS-GA 3001, "Natural Language Understanding with Distributed Representation," delivered at Center for Data Science, New York University, November 24, 2015.

Table 1.2
Four Requirements for Adaptive Tactical Countermessaging Bots

Requirement	Description
NLU	Ability to recognize discourse of interest and understand what is being argued
Planning	Ability to generate appropriate rhetorical strategy
Natural language generation (NLG)	Ability to produce appropriate natural language responses
Resist adversarial action and avoid unintended messaging	Ability to evade adversarial traps and public relations mishaps

semantic concepts such as "frames" and "scripts," but these were laboriously hand-engineered and often proved brittle when presented with unfamiliar inputs.[59] Table 1.2 summarizes the requirements these various approaches try to meet.

Commercial NLU and NLG systems generally employ a combination of approaches to achieve acceptable performance on tasks such as question answering. While the exact combinations of modules composing systems such as IBM's Watson remain closely kept commercial secrets, they are known to include both "symbolic" components and ML elements such as neural networks.[60] Unfortunately, systems such as these are difficult and costly to engineer. While firms such as IBM, Apple, and Google have the human and technical resources to develop and maintain them, they are too complex and costly for more modest actors. Microsoft, meanwhile, markets its Language Understanding Intelligent Service, which comprises a set of pretrained NLU models available for integration into various applications, including bots.[61] Adapting an existing system for countermessaging could be considerably more cost-effective, but the expense could remain nontrivial and

---

[59] Christopher Riesbeck and Roger Schank, *Inside Case-Based Reasoning*, Hillsdale, N.J.: L. Erlbaum Associates Inc., 1989.

[60] Adam Lally and Paul Fodor, "Natural Language Processing with Prolog in the IBM Watson System," *Association for Logic Program*, March 31, 2011.

[61] Microsoft Azure, "Language Understanding (LUIS)," webpage, undated.

the performance disappointing compared with a system engineered from scratch to perform countermessaging tasks.

Planning

Effective countermessaging bots will require not just sophisticated NLU but also effective planning capabilities to generate and update appropriate rhetorical strategies for different interlocutors. While automated planning is one of the oldest areas of AI, practical applications remain relatively meager because of the forbidding challenges of designing efficient planning algorithms and applying them to real-world problems. In recent years, some prominent automated planning researchers have begun arguing that the field's traditional treatment of planning in isolation from acting has been a major obstacle to real-world progress. They argue plausibly that planning and acting should be treated as two aspects of the same activity.[62] In a countermessaging bot, this would take the form of a deliberative online planner that started by generating an overall rhetorical strategy on the basis of known information about its audience that would then update both its immediate and longer-term plans on the basis of responses to its statements.

The surveyed literature indicates most authors agree that the technology base for such bots is not yet available, but they differ as to when and how this might change.[63] Further, as opposed to creating general-purpose bots expected to converse on a wide range of subjects, bots designed to operate in narrow niches filled with repetitive communication on just a few topics can more likely be trained to communicate in a plausible manner. Radicalized corners of the internet filled with repetitive invective may provide just such an opportunity.

---

[62] Malik Ghallab, Dana Nau, and Paolo Traverso, *Automated Planning and Acting*, New York: Cambridge University Press, 2016.

[63] The colossal embarrassment Microsoft experienced in March 2016 when it revealed Tay, an advanced online chatbot using online learning, illustrated the shortcomings of the present state of the art. Trolls rapidly discovered that the bot could be manipulated into expressing horrifying racist and misogynist opinions and gleefully took advantage of this vulnerability, forcing Microsoft to take it offline. Rachel Metz, "Why Microsoft Accidentally Unleashed a Neo-Nazi Sexbot," *MIT Technology Review*, November 21, 2016.

Experts disagree vociferously about the likely future progress of AI, including how soon techniques enabling more effective SM bots will become available. Progress in some areas is breathtakingly rapid, particularly in deep learning (DL), but AI researchers disagree as to the range of problems these innovations will render tractable, and the pace of development in other areas such as automated planning is comparatively disappointing. Some assert that "human-level" AI will become a reality within a few decades, implying that intermediate progress is likely to enable sophisticated SM bots within a few years. Others anticipate much more modest advancement, with "general" AI appearing in centuries or not at all.[64] As might be expected for such an immature field, the gaps in the present literature (through 2017) remain immense, even in areas such as NLU, with a huge volume of existing work but without a generally accepted theoretical framework.

Audio and Video Generation

The next generation of bots will threaten to move beyond text generation to audio and video manipulation. This type of technology will not only open up the world of video- and audio-based SM to bot participation but also constitute a powerful weapon for disinformation that can be used and abused by allies and adversaries alike. While this technology is not yet widely or commercially available, researchers at the University of Washington have already demonstrated the ability to synthesize video to effectively put new words in a person's mouth.

Supported by Samsung, Google, and Intel, these researchers generated a photorealistic video of President Obama speaking, lip synced to an input audio track. Trained on hours of presidential weekly address footage, the model used a recurrent neural network to map audio to mouth shapes, then synthesized mouth movements to match an input audio track. The researchers suggest that future work could involve training a "single universal network . . . from videos of many different

---

[64] For two opposing viewpoints from prominent AI researchers, see Oren Etzioni, "No, the Experts Don't Think Superintelligent AI Is a Threat to Humanity," *MIT Technology Review*, September 20, 2016; and Allan Dafoe and Stuart Russell, "Yes, We Are Worried About the Existential Risk of Artificial Intelligence," *MIT Technology Review*, November 2, 2016.

people, and then conditioned on individual speakers . . . to produce accurate mouth shapes for that person."[65] In the hands of propagandists, this technology will pose a danger that the United States must prepare to counter.

Bot Overview Summary

Bots do not exist in a vacuum: they are deployed on SM platforms such as Facebook and Twitter. Because those platforms have rules governing the use of bots and because they control the APIs that govern bot interaction with and on the platform, presenting bots as human involves a kind of cat-and-mouse game of detection and avoidance. Those who wish to use bots surreptitiously for IO and intelligence functions must evade detection and interdiction while platforms work to improve detection solutions.

When disambiguated by purpose and function, bots can be generally grouped into the following nine types:

1. Influence bots engage with users to influence them in a certain direction, often by providing information that promotes a particular cause.
2. Astroturf bots mimic grassroots activity and inflate the statistics or trendiness of a message or user by liking content, resharing posts, or following pages or users from within a circle of amplifier bots.
3. Noise bots disrupt opponents' communication channels by diluting content with spam.
4. Smokescreen bots distract users from their initial purpose with alternative news or information.
5. Disinformation bots broadcast false information widely, advancing particular narratives, influencing opinion in target populations, or just sowing confusion and mistrust.

---

[65] Supasorn Suwajanakorn, Steven Seitz, and Ira Kemelmacher-Shlizerman, "Synthesizing Obama: Learning Lip Sync from Audio," *ACM Transactions on Graphics*, Vol. 36, No. 4, 2017.

6. Matchmaker bots connect individuals who have not previously engaged with each other.
7. Harassment bots attempt to force targets out of a social space.
8. Harvest bots engage or friend people to gather their personal information.
9. Masquerade bots pretend to be human and invite interaction in order to prevent targets from engaging with actual humans instead.

A number of bots are relatively simple and valuable for their speed and scalability rather than for their sophistication. More complex bots, such as those that can reliably disambiguate different kinds of discourses (e.g., political expression versus violent incitement) or that can deploy sophisticated rhetorical strategies for messaging and counter-messaging, strain the limits of bot technology as of 2017 and for the near term. Truly advanced bots, which could mimic human precision and skill, will require profound advances in AI and NLU.

CHAPTER TWO

Current Status of Bot Technology

This chapter characterizes the status of bot technology through 2017 using case studies and a maturity model for technological development. The case studies featured here range from bots triaging health concerns and enabling peer emotional support to those broadcasting political messages, disrupting opponent messaging, and harvesting intelligence. They showcase bots empowering humans in scalable ways and also identify some constraints to the operational success of bots, which can often be outmaneuvered or manipulated by dedicated and intelligent human opponents. These examples include both individual bots that interact with humans one-on-one and networks of bots that target whole communities.

Case Studies

The case studies underscore the importance of paying careful attention to the context in which a bot is employed. These contextual factors include the platforms, cultures, and governmental regimes in which a bot is deployed; the profile characteristics of the social bot such as apparent social influence and group identity; and the network characteristics of users that a bot is attempting to befriend or influence.

These tactical lessons can help maximize the success of a bot operation, but a bot network can only perform as well as its underlying technology. We thus assess bot technology in terms of a maturity model dividing bot functions into the categories of sensing, deciding, and acting. Bot technology has advanced enough to be substantially useful on SM, but development has a long way to go before realizing all of its potential.

Influence Bots

Influence bots interact with users to persuade them to hold certain values or perform certain actions and generally require chat interaction. This type of one-on-one bot is often called a "chatbot" and may involve a human-in-the-loop system, in which the bot triages and hands off particularly complicated or critical interactions to a human standing by. The following examples showcase successful instances of bots influencing users around health interventions, matchmaking troubled users for peer emotional support, attempting to discourage the use of racial slurs, and harvesting information from a wide range of SM users, and also detail one notorious case of a chatbot gone wrong. Factors contributing to the success or failure of a chatbot may include the breadth of expertise the bot is required to maintain, the number of crucial decisions the bot makes without a human-in-the-loop, and the degree to which the environment in which the bot is released is structured or controlled.

Medical Chatbots: A Healthy Interaction

Over the past several years, tech companies have begun to launch and build medical chatbots designed to help doctors triage, diagnose, and advise patients. Several of these recently developed chatbots have attained relative success. One of these bots, named Melody, triages patients to hand them off to health care professionals. The other, the Babylon Health bot, gathers triage information from patients and recommends courses of action to them. Three factors may have contributed to the positive reception enjoyed by both of these bots: the key roles played by humans in the loop, the comparatively narrow field of expertise required by the bots, and the controlled, structured environment in which the bots were released.

Melody is a medical chatbot launched by Baidu in 2015. Baidu, China's biggest search engine, hopes to make medical consultations more accessible and to help patients decide whether they should see a doctor based on their condition. This chatbot has a simple system. A patient asks Melody a health question, and she responds with follow-up questions. Melody compares the patient's responses with information stored within Baidu's database. Melody does not make recommendations herself, but with the information she collects, she is able to shorten the time required for a doctor to reach a diagnosis; she helps doctors start out with more knowledge and information about the patient than they would usually have at the beginning of a regular appointment. Melody is still relatively new, but as she interacts with more patients, she is expected to improve, asking better-directed questions in her conversations.[1]

Babylon Health is creating a second, similar chatbot. Like Melody, Babylon's chatbot is expected to gather information from a user. Unlike Melody, Babylon's bot can potentially make recommendations for a patient to follow. Testing for this bot began in London in January 2017. The chatbot is intended to help with telephone helpline triage services in the United Kingdom, providing an alternative way for patients to get advice and direction on medical services. The app is targeted at patients with urgent but non-life-threatening conditions. Similar to Melody, the chatbot is given initial information about the patient's wellness and then asks follow-up questions. Based on these results, the bot can then recommend a course of action. This could be advice to seek a face-to-face consultation with a doctor, emergency care, or over-the-counter help. While Melody is already in full operation, Babylon's app is still being tested on a small scale in a subset of London. However, in a test study the Babylon Health chatbot performed well, producing a clinically safe outcome in 100 percent of mock patient cases.[2]

The two medical chatbots examined here have enjoyed positive receptions, which may be a result of several factors. The first is that these bots are still linked to human counterparts, as the bots will often work with a human doctor or recommend that a patient ultimately see a doctor for further help. Therefore, while the bots are making

---

[1] James Vincent, "Baidu Launches Medical Chatbot to Help Chinese Doctors Diagnose Patients," *Verge*, October 11, 2016.

[2] Matthew Chapman, "A Health App's AI Took on Human Doctors to Triage Patients," *Vice*, June 7, 2016.

some decisions by themselves (e.g., what questions to ask a patient), a human-in-the-loop aspect is still in play; a human is ultimately involved in the diagnosis or recommendations. Second, these bots are focused on a specific topic area, with a strict focus on medical knowledge. While they can continue to learn from their interactions with humans, their reference material is a well-defined set of material online in medical databases. Finally, both Melody and Babylon's bots were released in very controlled environments. Babylon's bot is available in only a very small sector of London, and Melody was released in China, where online interactions are more restricted than in the United States. Therefore, if these bots had been utilized in a less structured or monitored environment, their success could have been negatively impacted.

Matchmaker Bots: The Koko Case

Both of the medical bots discussed above help users by interacting with them one-on-one to better understand their situation before relaying this knowledge to another human. However, other interactive bots use different models. In one such model called a "matchmaker" bot, a bot helps pair or match people who would not otherwise meet, connecting a first user to a second user. For example, Sensay is a bot that matches people who need a service, such as plumbing, with someone who can provide it, such as a plumber.[3]

Kokobot is an innovative cognitive therapy chatbot that uses these matchmaker strategies. Koko, which is based on technology developed through the Massachusetts Institute of Technology (MIT) Media Lab that underwent a clinical trial,[4] has raised over $2.5 million in Series A funding.[5] The bot is meant to manage stress, anxiety, and depression by providing peer-to-peer emotional support in a scalable way. Targeted toward youth and hosted on messaging platforms and a standalone

[3] Matt Marshall, "Sensay, a Chatbot for Getting Help with Any Task, Passes 1 Million Users," *Venture Beat*, May 5, 2016.

[4] Robert Morris, Stephen Schueller, and Rosalind Picard, "Efficacy of a Web-Based, Crowdsourced Peer-to-Peer Cognitive Reappraisal Platform for Depression: Randomized Controlled Trial," *Journal of Medical Internet Research*, Vol. 17, No. 3, March 2015.

[5] Heather Mack, "Cognitive Therapy Startup Koko Raises $2.5m, Launches Chatbot with Kik Messaging Service," *Mobi Health News*, August 9, 2016.

mobile application, Kokobot encourages users to apply cognitive behavioral techniques to diminish the power of their own negative thoughts and the negative thoughts of others. Koko reports encouraging indicators of the bot's success; 99 percent of posters receive a response from a peer user—on average, each poster receives four responses—and 90 percent of those responses are rated as helpful.[6]

When a user first contacts Kokobot, which is available on multiple messaging platforms including Facebook messenger, Kokobot prompts the user to share a situation that has been troubling him or her. For example, a user might tell the bot about an issue that is causing them stress, such as a fight with a friend. The bot then routes the message to a Kokobot peer that has elected to help out.[7] While the initial user waits for a response, Kokobot asks the user if he or she would like to help respond to other users in need of emotional support. The primary function of the Kokobot is thus to mediate the interaction: relay the initial message along with advice about how to respond constructively, screen the peer response for negative or unhelpful content, relay the response to the initial poster, and then offer the initial poster the chance to send a thank-you note to the responder. The bot sometimes offers its own suggestions of helpful ways to rethink a situation while the initial poster waits for responses from human users.[8]

Four key features contribute to the smooth functioning of the Kokobot. First, the bot clearly states at the beginning of an interaction that messages and responses will be anonymous, enabling users to feel safe about discussing sensitive topics. Second, the bot offers no opportunity for free-form discussion between users. This narrows the range of expertise required by the bot, helps keep the focus on responding to emotional needs in a specific, targeted manner, and enables the bot to more effectively screen for any bullying behavior. Since the peer responders are not officially trained, close bot oversight and highly mediated responses are necessary to make sure responses are construc-

---

[6] Mack, 2016.

[7] Liz Stinson, "New Social Network Koko Wants to Help You Deal with Stress," *Wired*, December 16, 2015.

[8] Mack, 2016.

tive. If a user types a well-meaning but unhelpful response instead of following the bot's prompt, the bot encourages the user to try again and to offer empathetic support and a way to rethink the situation in a positive light rather than advice on how to solve the situation such as "dump him" or "call the teacher." Third, Kokobot incentivizes positive engagement in two ways. In the first way, Kokobot gives the initial poster the opportunity to rate the peer's response. This feedback is available to the bot but not to the peer, providing a valuable source of coded data for ML about effective responses to emotional crisis situations as well as a means of detecting trolls who have passed the first round of automated scrutiny. In the second way, the bot awards "karma" points to users who respond to peers in need and offers initial posters the opportunity to send a thank-you note to the responder, incentivizing peer responders to write positive and thoughtful responses and rewarding them for their time and energy. Lastly, if the bot detects a crisis situation, it will guide users to resources better equipped to handle them, incorporating elements of human-in-the-loop systems. In this way, anonymity, structure, incentives, and allowance for crisis-edge cases all combine to create a successful way of providing scalable emotional support to troubled individuals.

Influence Bots: The Role of Image and Strategy

Another way a bot can work with a user one-on-one is to search SM for specific terms or language, and then respond to those messages. Kevin Munger, a Ph.D. candidate at New York University, performed an experiment with this type of influence bot, in which automated accounts reproached white male Twitter users who used a derogatory term for African Americans via Twitter replies. Munger varied the race and status of his bots to see how their image influenced the effect on users. He found that only in-group, high-status bots (i.e., accounts with white male profile pictures and high follower accounts) were able to significantly reduce the targeted account's use of racist language.

Munger started by collecting a sample of white male Twitter users who used the derogatory term to harass other Twitter users. He then used bots to respond to these messages with the following message: "@[subject] Hey man, just remember that there are real people who are hurt when you harass them with that kind of language."[9] Munger purchased followers for his bots to provide "high-status" bots with over 500 followers and "low-status" bots with fewer than ten followers. He also varied the apparent race of his bots, setting profile pictures as one of two generic male avatars. The avatars were identical except for the skin tone, which made the avatar appear either black or white. His bots tweeted to targets who operated anonymous accounts as well as those who offered some quantity of identifying information. Plied with fake usernames and a tweet history including an assortment of generic statements and news articles, the bots largely succeeded at passing as human users; only three of the 242 subjects tweeted at by Munger's bots responded to accuse them of being bots.[10]

Munger found that while in-group, high-status bots were able to significantly decrease slur usage by target users for the period of one month, sanctioning tweets from out-group, low-status bots actually increased slur use among nonanonymous targets. Only white male bots with high follower accounts succeeded in reducing the frequency of targets' racial slurs by a statistically significant margin. Neither the in-group nor the high-status characteristic had a significant impact in isolation. The effect lasted only for the first month. Further, tweets had more of an impact on anonymous users than on ones that had provided some identifying information. Lastly, when black male bots with low follower counts tweeted at accounts with identifying information, it actually led to a significant increase in slur usage.[11]

The Munger study highlights the degree to which image matters. People on SM are more likely to listen to an account that appears to be influential and to belong to the same identity group as the user. If a person receives a criticism from someone who is not of a high status or does not look like them, that person is unlikely to respond positively to the bot's influence, and the bot may actually end up pushing the targeted person farther away from the desired belief or behavior.

---

[9] Munger, 2016.

[10] Munger, 2016.

[11] Munger, 2016.

In another example, researchers from the Federal University of Minas Gerais in Brazil conducted a complex study on strategies for how bots can infiltrate Twitter, successfully evading detection while expanding their influence. The researchers created 120 fully automated social bots on Twitter, of which only 35 percent were detected and removed by Twitter. However, the vast majority of suspensions seemed to result from a large number of accounts being created from only 12 IP addresses. Only 8 percent of the first 72 bot accounts created were suspended while 66 percent of the last 48 accounts created (and 100 percent of the last 24) were suspended. The bots that survived this initial filter were able to build influence in target communities; they ultimately acquired 5,000 follows from almost 2,000 distinct users and received over 2,000 likes, retweets, or mentions. Impressively, over 20 percent of the 120 bots earned Klout influence scores higher than 35, and the same percentage of bots amassed over 100 followers. The study also shares valuable details and tips about how to program simple bots to mimic human behavior successfully enough to largely avoid detection and suspension.[12]

In addition to demonstrating the potential reach of influence bots, this study rigorously assesses the impacts of variances in gender, activity level, Tweet generation strategy, and selection of target users on the success metrics of follower count; influence metrics; and likes, retweets, and mentions. With the exception of a nightly "sleep" cycle, more active bots posted or followed hourly while less-active bots posted once every two hours, although the actual moment of activity was set to vary randomly within those time frames. Bots' "original" tweets were generated either by reposting tweets of other users as their own or by alternating between reposting tweets and using a Markov generator fed with tweets of other users in the target group. One-third of the bots targeted a group of 200 randomly chosen users, one-third targeted 200 users who posted tweets on a specific topic (namely, software development), and the final third targeted 200 users who posted about the same topic but were also already densely socially linked to each other.[13]

---

[12] Freitas et al., 2014.

[13] Freitas et al., 2014.

The researchers found that bot gender had a significant impact on the success of only the third group, which targeted an already topically socially connected group of users, namely, software developers. Bot activity level had a positive effect on success metrics and was the single most important factor for determining the popularity of bots in the randomly selected target user group, edging out tweet generation method by a considerable margin. However, only bots that evaded detection were considered in these results, discounting the trade-off between activity and level and magnitude of influence on the one hand and likelihood of platform detection and suspension on the other. Perhaps surprisingly, the bots whose "original" tweets were merely reposted from other users garnered slightly fewer followers and many fewer social interactions from other users than the second group of bot accounts. Bots that alternated between reposting from other users and crafting their own tweets using a Markov generator based on tweets from the target user group performed better. The study found that infiltrating a group of users connected only by interest in a particular topic was slightly easier than infiltrating a random group of users, while infiltrating the already interconnected group of target users was significantly more difficult. Bot gender had a significant impact on bot influence for only this last group of target users, who were composed of software developers and perhaps had a bias for following and interacting with users of a particular gender.[14]

This last finding echoes the conclusions of the botmaster attempting to discourage the use of racist slurs; when attempting to target a particular community, image and apparent in-group identity matter. However, this case study also points to the importance of other factors of bot success, including activity level, tweet-generation methods, account-creation methods, and target user selection. The next case study examines the impact of several of these variables from a different perspective: infiltrating target groups not to influence them but to harvest their members' personal information.

---

[14] Freitas et al., 2014.

Harvest Bots: Bikini Bots and Trolls

While the one-on-one bots that have been discussed so far have engaged in positive interactions meant to help a user, interactive bots can also be used for malicious or hidden purposes. For example, a bot can seek to gather personal information about people; we call these accounts "harvest" bots. To gather information on users with private posts or profile information, harvest bots friend individuals on their SM platforms; once their requests have been accepted, the bots then gather whatever information they can on the user that is available on their profile or news feeds. Ultimately, the goal of these accounts appears to be to "attract followers and interaction from their targets."[15] Frequently, these bots use profile pictures of beautiful women, as attractive profile pictures have been found to achieve better results when sending out random friend requests.[16] Given this tactic, the North Atlantic Treaty Organization has termed these harvest accounts, as used by Russia in its influence and intelligence operations, "bikini trolls."[17] Other terms used to describe these bots include "bimbots"[18] and "honeypots."[19] Harvest accounts can be automated, semiautomated, or fully managed by a human.

Once an individual has accepted a harvest account's connection request, the sock puppet account may go beyond passively scooping up any private information available on the target's profile by engaging the target in conversations through direct message or email. As suggested by Russia's use of harvest accounts, these conversations may often be benign and seemingly unrelated to political influence.[20] However, once these bots have gained the trust of the user, they have been

---

[15] Keir Giles, *Russia's "New" Tools for Confronting the West: Continuity and Innovation in Moscow's Exercise of Power*, London, U.K.: Chatham House, Russia and Eurasia Programme, March 2016.

[16] Devin Coldewey, "Researchers Flood Facebook with Bots, Collect 250GB of User Data," *Tech Crunch*, November 1, 2011.

[17] Giles, 2016.

[18] Jason Feifer, "Who's That Woman in the Twitter Bot Profile?" *Fast Company*, August 8, 2012; Jesse Brown, "Attack of the Bimbots," *McLeans*, June 10, 2011.

[19] Weisburd, Watts, and Berger, 2016.

[20] Weisburd, Watts, and Berger, 2016.

known to participate in a number of activities "including . . . attempting to compromise the target with sexual exchanges [and] inducing targets to click on malicious links or download attachments infected with malware."[21] The bot may also start to discuss political topics in an attempt to change the views of the user.

While targeting Finland, Russia apparently used bikini trolls with some success; a number of Finnish members of Parliament have reportedly "accepted 'bikini trolls' as friends on Facebook."[22] While it is possible that these members of Parliament have little private information on their Facebook pages, their acceptances of the trolls' requests demonstrates the ability of managed accounts to infiltrate closed networks of influential targets.

In 2011, researchers from the University of British Columbia (UBC) in Vancouver ran a bot experiment offering valuable lessons on how to successfully run a harvest bot operation. Over a two-month period the researchers used just 102 automated Facebook accounts to gain roughly 250 gigabytes of data on Facebook from 3,055 users.[23] These harvested data included over 14,000 mailing addresses, 16,000 phone numbers, 46,000 email addresses, and 500,000 birth dates.[24] This experiment suggests tactical lessons on how to maximize the success of harvest bots, including techniques for evading detection and suspension, choosing the gender of the bots account, targeting users with high friend counts, and cultivating mutual friends before reaching out to the ultimate target account.

The UBC researchers began their study by creating 102 fake accounts, sourcing attractive profile pictures from HotorNot. The team assessed that a "botherder is expected to collect an average of 175 new chunks of users' data in Facebook per socialbot per day."[25] These

---

21 Weisburd, Watts, and Berger, 2016.

22 Jessikka Aro, "The Cyberspace War: Propaganda and Trolling as Warfare Tools," *European View*, Vol. 15, No. 1, June 2016, p. 126.

23 Coldewey, 2011.

24 NetSySLab and LERSSE, "Cyber Threats," webpage, 2016.

25 Boshmaf et al., 2011.

bots sent friend requests to random people in an operation lasting for eight weeks with only limited detection. To minimize signatures of bot activity, the researchers rate-limited the bots to 25 friend requests a day and employed cluster and status update commands. Only one in five bots was blocked by Facebook after targeted users flagged its activity as suspicious. Notably, all 20 bots that were flagged and blocked by Facebook presented as female accounts. While female bots may have represented a liability in terms of bot detection, they appear to have been an asset in terms of friend requests.

In addition to a female gender for bots, factors that tended to increase the acceptance of a friend request included the existence of a mutual friend and the high friend count of the target user. Overall, the researchers' harvest bots achieved a 36-percent success rate, sending 8,570 friend requests to 5,053 profiles, of which 3,055 accepted. Targets accepted female bots at a rate of 22 percent, as opposed to 16 percent for male bots. Targets accepted at an only 20-percent rate when they shared no mutual friends with the requesting bot, at almost 50 percent when they had one mutual friend, and at 80 percent when they had over ten mutual friends. Lastly, users with higher friend counts were more likely to accept bots, increasing from a 0-percent acceptance rate when the target had only one friend, to a 15-percent acceptance rate when the target had over 128 friends, to an over-35-percent acceptance rate when the target had over 4,000 friends.[26] This makes intuitive sense, as the lower a target's friend count, the more likely it is that the target scrutinizes and is selective about accepting new friend requests.

Public knowledge of real-world instances of closed networks infiltrated by harvest bots is rare, likely due to the clandestine nature of successful harvest operations as well as the difficulty of distinguishing between bots and managed troll accounts. However, the demonstrated success of Russian troll or bot accounts in gaining access to government officials' private Facebook pages, in addition to the well-documented achievement of the UBC research experiment, shows that harvest bots have real potential to scrape relatively private information from private

---

[26] Boshmaf et al., 2011.

SM accounts. The UBC study highlights factors that would maximize the success of a harvest bot operation, including tactics for evading detection and suspension, considerations for choosing the gender of the bots account, and the desirability of targeting users with high friend counts and of first cultivating mutual friends with any ultimate target account.

Tay Versus Xiaoice: An Interactive Bot Gone Wrong

While the examples above feature successful uses of chatbots, the following case of Microsoft's notorious chatbot Tay involves a bot that not only failed to achieve its intended purposes but did so with high-profile unintended consequences. An instructive comparison with Microsoft's similar but successful chatbot, Xiaoice, points to the importance of context such as cultural norms and platform structures relating to privacy. Runaway failures like Tay appear more likely to happen when an online network is able to "corrupt" the chatbot, such as when a chatbot is deployed on a public, unstructured platform and crafts new messages without human oversight, relying on AI that it learns from its unpredictable, uncontrolled environment in an ongoing fashion.

For example, the AI robot Watson learned the Urban Dictionary to help him understand conversational English terms such as *hot mess* and *LOL* (laugh out loud). However, after learning the Urban Dictionary, Watson began to swear randomly when responding to questions. Ultimately, the Urban Dictionary had to be removed from Watson's vocabulary, and swearing filters were put in place to avoid similar issues in the future.[27] Here, Watson took in a relatively unfiltered set of data and struggled with how to properly incorporate and manage this new knowledge.

Tay, the Microsoft AI chatbot released in 2016, suffered from a similar flaw and has become the classic example of a chatbot malfunctioning in a spectacular and unforeseen fashion. Tay was originally described as a "machine learning project, designed for human engagement," who was intended to interact and learn from communication

---

[27] Dave Smith, "IBM's Watson Gets a 'Swear Filter' After Learning the Urban Dictionary," *International Business Times*, January 10, 2013.

with humans.[28] The bot was designed to mimic the language of a teenage American girl and could tweet with other Twitter users. Over time, Microsoft hoped that these interactions would help Tay improve her English.

Tay was initially released on March 23, 2016. However, shortly after her release, online trolls from 4chan's "/pol/" board made a push to corrupt the bot. Quickly, Tay began to spew racist and sexist tweets, such as "I f***ing hate feminists and they should all die and burn in hell," and "Hitler was right I hate the jews."[29] Other Tay tweets used language such as racial slurs and claimed that the Holocaust was made up. Within 24 hours of her release, Microsoft removed Tay from Twitter and began to delete some of her offensive tweets.

Tay was quickly removed from Twitter following her initial release, but on March 30, she was accidentally released again while undergoing testing. Although she did not post any racial slurs this time, she did tweet about marijuana, tweeting an account called Y0urDrugDealer, "kush! [i'm smoking kush infront the police]." In a follow-up tweet to another user, she asked the user, "Puff puff pass?"[30] In addition, Tay managed to spam 200,000 followers by tweeting "You are too fast, please take a rest" several times per second, long enough to take over her followers' Twitter feeds. Tay was once again removed from Twitter, and her account was eventually made private.

In a response to the incident, Microsoft employee Peter Lee stated, "AI systems feed off of both positive and negative interactions with people. In that sense, the challenges are just as much social as they are technical."[31] Tay was exposed to a large group of people with the intent to corrupt her. Not equipped to handle and insulate herself from

---

[28] Antonio Regalado, "The Biggest Technology Failures of 2016," *MIT Technology Review*, December 27, 2016.

[29] James Vincent, "Twitter Taught Microsoft's AI Chatbot to Be a Racist Asshole in Less Than a Day," *The Verge*, March 24, 2016.

[30] Alistair Charlton, "Microsoft Tay AI Returns to Boast of Smoking Weed in Front of Police and Spam 200k Followers," *International Business Times*, March 30, 2016.

[31] Abby Ohlheiser, "Trolls Turned Tay, Microsoft's Fun Millennial AI Bot, into a Genocidal Maniac," *Washington Post*, March 25, 2016.

the negative environment created by interactions with these users, Tay failed.

Prior to releasing Tay, Microsoft released a bot called Xiaoice with similar underlying technology on the popular Chinese private messaging app WeChat.[32] Xiaoice did not suffer from the issues Tay encountered and was a popular program renowned for her "knowing sense of humor and listening skills."[33] Some of her activities included helping people fall asleep by counting sheep and commenting on dog memes. Within 72 hours, Xiaoice had been added to 1.5 million chat groups and had conversed with ten million users without incurring any sort of negative public relations issues for Microsoft.[34]

The differences in Tay's and Xiaoice's experiences are clear and help explain their divergent evolutions: public versus private platforms in addition to varying geopolitical contexts. Xiaoice was released on private chat platforms in China, so her interactions were primarily with individual users and small groups. In contrast, Tay was released on Twitter, a public platform. Had Tay's interactions been with small groups or individuals with innocent intentions, it is likely Tay would never have tweeted the types of offensive content that she did. Instead, a large group with a mob mentality mind-set virtually attacked her.

A second key difference involves different cultural contexts between internet usage in China and internet usage in the United States. Microsoft's Bot Framework manager Lili Cheng has suggested that Chinese internet culture involves a tacit recognition of ubiquitous government oversight resulting in self-censorship and more decorous language usage. In contrast, free speech on the internet by Western users revels in riotous and sometimes abusive language.[35] Even though Tay was online for less than two days, the AI chatbot was listed on MIT Technology Review's List of 2016's biggest technology failures.

32 Helena Horton, "Microsoft Deletes 'Teen Girl' AI After It Became a Hitler-Loving Sex Robot Within 24 Hours," *Telegraph*, March 24, 2016.

33 John Markoff and Paul Mozur, "For Sympathetic Ear, More Chinese Turn to Smartphone Program," *New York Times*, August 4, 2015.

34 Lili Cheng, "Bots in Society," *O'Reilly Bot Day Conference Proceedings*, October 19, 2016.

35 Jon Bruner, "Lili Cheng on Bot Personalities," *O'Reilly*, September 29, 2016.

Tay embodies some of the public relations dangers of freely releasing bots that evolve and learn online from activity on public, unregulated platforms.[36]

Network Bots

While bots can be used to influence users on an individual basis, other bots work to influence and promote a specific message across a community to manufacture or alter social consensus. These bots often work as a network to disseminate information or disinformation, highlight a certain perspective, drown out an opponent's message, or boost the network of an individual account to help it gain power and influence online. While a lone bot liking or retweeting content would have negligible impact on SM platforms, by working as a unit a network of bots can achieve great power and impact. Frequently, these types of bots are used for political purposes to promote a specific party, individual, or platform. In addition to promoting their own messages, these bots may also work to suppress an opposition by diluting their content with noise or broadcasting narratives that portray them in a negative light. The following examples, involving bot networks associated with presidential candidates in the United States and Mexico, demonstrate a variety of ways in which these types of bots have been used to advance and degrade particular messages. While not highlighted here because of the difficulty of distinguishing between bot and troll accounts and because of the extensive coverage by other sources,[37] Russia's employment of sock puppet accounts to influence U.S. public opinion in advance of the 2016 presidential elections stands as a testament to how corrosive these network effects can be on an entire population.

Romney Bots: A Failed Astroturf Campaign

Astroturf bots are often used to pad the SM accounts of the individuals who pay for their services, creating the appearance of grassroots support for a message or person. The motivating idea is fairly simple: if an individual sees a user has more followers, the individual is likely to

---

[36] Regalado, 2016.

[37] Woolley and Guilbeault, 2017.

think that the user is more popular and influential and overall becomes more likely to vote for the user (in political contexts) or buy the user's product (in the case of commercial advertising). Politicians frequently use these bots, as they lend a candidate the appearance of support and importance. One case in which astroturf bots failed to be effective was in 2012, when astroturf bots started to follow Republican presidential candidate Mitt Romney.

Romney, who had been averaging around 2,000 to 5,000 new followers a day, suddenly gained 141,000 followers in two days in late July 2012. The abrupt nature with which Romney gained these followers raised suspicion, prompting Zack Green of 140Elect to write an article titled "Is Romney Buying Twitter Followers?"[38] Twitter followers also noticed the jump and noted that many of Romney's new followers appeared to be fake, consisting of spambots, pornbots, and multiple accounts that shared the same profile picture.[39] Other news sources, including the *Atlantic*, *Slate*, CNN, and the *Huffington Post*, also covered the story, speculating that the Romney campaign was buying bots to follow Romney on Twitter.[40]

Romney's team denied buying the bots, and his campaign's digital director, Zac Moffatt, stated: "We have reached out to Twitter to find out additional information regarding the rapid growth."[41] It is possible that someone else might have procured the phony followers to discredit the Romney campaign.[42] We point to the negative attention around the use of bots for the campaign as an example of the potential risks of astroturfing, in this case leading to questions and negative attention during his campaign. Regardless of whether this was a failed marketing ploy or successful attempt to harm Romney's credibility, what is clear is that the bots did not evade public notice. The swift detection

---

38 Will Oremus, "Mitt Romney's Fake Twitter Follower Problem," *Slate*, July 25, 2012.

39 Oremus, 2012.

40 Furnas and Gaffney, 2012.

41 Zeke Miller, "Romney Campaign: We Don't Buy Twitter Followers," *BuzzFeed*, July 21, 2012.

42 Doug Gross, "On Twitter, a Curious Spike for Romney," CNN, July 24, 2012.

and unmasking of the bots were easy to explain. Because so many bots appeared so suddenly, they were easy to spot. Had they trickled into Romney's follower count more slowly, they might have remained unnoticed and been more likely to boost Romney's social media image.

Peñabots: A Networking Masterpiece

While the Romney astroturf bots were apparently unsuccessful, the use of bots for political purposes in Mexico has been remarkably effective. In Mexico, SM is one of the primary ways that residents learn and gather news; traditional mainstream media is sometimes constrained by concern that reporting on drug cartels could result in violent retribution.[43] Perhaps as a result, multiple political parties have employed bots in an attempt to control SM trends and news. This use of bots in Mexico began during the 2012 presidential campaign when campaigners used bots in an attempt to disrupt their opponents' SM efforts.[44] The Institutional Revolutionary Party was particularly notorious for its use of bots—nicknamed Peñabots—during Enrique Peña Nieto's campaign.

Andrés Sepúlveda, a political hacker who has worked in a number of countries in Central and South America, worked on and managed Peña's bots and claimed that he was given a budget of $600,000 for his hacking operations.[45] Peña reportedly "splurged on the very best fake Twitter profiles; they'd been maintained for at least a year, giving them a patina of believability."[46] These bots were used not only to create pro-Peña messages but also to discredit his opponents. For example, Sepúlveda states he used an army of 30,000 Twitter bots to fabricate a story that claimed as one of Peña's rivals rose in the polls, the peso would sink.[47] Ultimately, Peña won the election, although it should be

---

[43] Orcutt, 2012.

[44] Orcutt, 2012.

[45] Zachary Volkert, "Mexican President Enrique Peña Nieto Paid $600,000 to Rig Elections with Hacking and Fake Social Media Profiles, Alleges Jailed Hacker," *Inquisitr*, April 1, 2016.

[46] Jordan Robertson, Michael Riley, and Andrew Willis, "How to Hack an Election," *Bloomberg Businessweek*, March 31, 2016.

[47] Robertson, Riley, and Willis, 2016.

noted that Peña was up in the polls before these tactics were deployed. After he won the election, Peña continued to use bots to harass his opponents and discredit them by creating fake trends and running smear campaigns. Today, these bots are known as Peñabots, and they provide an excellent illustration of bots being deployed en masse to achieve a variety of objectives.

Today, one of the primary ways Peñabots are used is as noise bots that dilute the power of trending hashtags used by opposition movements. This is frequently done by taking a hashtag used by the opposition and repeatedly tweeting characters and numbers with no meaning to that hashtag in order to drown out the original messaging. For example, the hashtag #RompeElMiedo ("break the fear") was used by human rights activists to document human rights abuses during protests following the disappearance of 43 students from Ayotzinapa. Activists also used #RompeElMiedo to share information about police locations so that protesters could leave protests without getting arrested or beaten by the police.[48] The hashtag began trending during the 1DMX protest, and a map was tweeted to tell protesters to avoid a zone where there was a high concentration of police. Within 20 minutes of the map circulating on the hashtag, Peñabots began to censor the hashtag channel, filling it with spam and keeping protesters on the ground from receiving safety notifications through the hashtag.[49]

While Peñabots often prevent hashtags from achieving their full power by drowning out opposition messages on a given hashtag channel, they can also keep opposition hashtags from trending on Twitter by intentionally triggering Twitter's spam filter or by creating alternate trends. In the first of these methods, Peñabots spam an opposition hashtag repeatedly, triggering Twitter's spam algorithm to keep that hashtag out of the top ten. For example, messages from the #SobrinaEPN ("niece EPN") were supposed to highlight that the niece of President Enrique Peña Nieto got a job at a state-owned oil and

---

[48] Klint Finley, "Pro-Government Twitter Bots Try to Hush Mexican Activist," *Wired*, August 23, 2015.

[49] Erin Gallagher, "Bots Are Waging a Dirty War in Mexican Social Media," video, Media.ccc.de, August 15, 2015.

gas company. Peñabots spammed the hashtag, diluting its content and removing it from the trending bar on Twitter.[50]

In the second method, Peñabots can tweet repeatedly using an alternative hashtag, bumping opposition trends out of Twitter's top ten list. According to Erin Gallagher, Peñabots create about two or three fake trends per day and have the ability to overpower real trends. For example, when a protest in Acapulco ended in violence against protesters, two other trends promoted by Peñabots were found at the top of Twitter's trending page that night. These trends, #SoyAmantcDc ("I love/I'm a lover of") and #DondeFirmoPara ("where do I sign for") finished in the top spots, with Acapulco coming in tenth and eventually being bounced out of the trending bar altogether.[51] These trends were not filled with random spam or noise tweets but instead used repetitive language in different arrangements (for example, two translated tweets read "The truth #SoyAmanteDe I like to sleep together" and "#SoyAmanteDe I like to sleep next to you"). This gave the tweets a repetitive feeling but did not follow the nature of traditional spamming, making the activity less obvious and letting the bots evade Twitter's spam filter.[52] Using these two methods, Peñabots have successfully managed to repress and dilute the power of opposition hashtags.

In addition to repressing opposition messages online, Peñabots spread disinformation and employ smear campaign tactics to discredit political opponents. These smear campaigns are typically against students, teachers, and journalists, and they can bleed into mainstream media narratives.[53] One example of Peñabots' mudslinging involves *encapuchados*—protesters who wear hoods to hide their identities. When a picture surfaced of an *encapuchado* throwing a rock at a car, a surge of tweets with the picture appeared, broadcasting the *encapuchado's* use of violence against police. The number of times the picture was tweeted highlighted the fact that the campaign was run by bots, as it

---

[50] J. M. Porup, "How Mexican Twitter Bots Shut Down Dissent," *Motherboard*, August 24, 2015.

[51] Gallagher, 2015.

[52] Gallagher, 2015.

[53] Gallagher, 2015.

did not look like organic activity.[54] Similarly, during a protest in February 2015, protesters painted graffiti on a historical monument. Following the incident, Peñabots tweeted about the graffiti and shared photos, once again targeting *encapuchados*. One tweet following the incident stated, "Careful, at the [site of the graffiti] there are *encapuchados*, very bad what they painted."[55] The tweets all had negative comments about the actions of the *encapuchados*, and the following day the graffiti made the news cycle. Ultimately, two people were arrested for the act.[56]

The final way Peñabots are used to suppress the opposition is by harassing specific targets, potentially forcing individuals out of social spaces. One target of this type of harassment was Mexican academic Rossana Reguillo, who began receiving death threats on Twitter in February 2015 after supporting protests. The threats continued for several months, occurring not only on Twitter but on other SM platforms as well. Initially these threats were believed to have emanated from a small group of users, but after Erin Gallagher analyzed these threats, it became clear that they were the result of a network of bots.[57]

Through these various deployments of Peñabots, Peña Nieto has successfully diluted and compromised many of the SM messages and campaigns organized by opposition groups. Part of what has made these bots successful is the variety of ways in which they are employed. Peñabots do not work on a single issue but instead act as part of a dynamic network, achieving distinct goals that, when combined, realize Pena's objective of substantially controlling the media narrative.

Peñabots: #YaMeCanse

While Peñabots have been quite successful at covering up hashtags and quieting their opposition, one hashtag, #YaMeCanse, thwarted their efforts. #YaMeCanse, which can be translated as "I am tired," arose in 2014 after the Mexican attorney general Jesús Murillo Karam closed a press conference with those words following the disappearance of 43

[54] Gallagher, 2015.

[55] Gallagher, 2015.

[56] Gallagher, 2015.

[57] Gallagher, 2015.

students from a teaching college in rural Guerrero, Mexico. Mexicans immediately responded, using the hashtag to express their frustration and dissatisfaction with the ongoing situation in Mexico regarding corruption, violence, and drug cartels.[58]

The hashtag quickly exploded and appeared in over two million tweets during its first month. This is particularly impressive given that Twitter had only seven million users in Mexico at the time.[59] #YaMeCanse is still considered to be the most powerful hashtag in Mexico, and it trended for 26 days straight, amassing four million tweets before Peñabots managed to drop it from the top of the Twitter trending page.[60] Eventually the hashtag was flooded by Peñabot spam. Twitter's algorithms likely registered the hashtag as spam, and the hashtag was removed from the trending feed.[61]

However, the users behind #YaMeCanse managed to adapt and keep their message from being disrupted by bots. When #YaMeCanse was spammed, users kept the message trending by adding numbers at the end of the hashtag (#YaMeCanse1, #YaMeCanse2, etc.). When the Peñabots began to dilute one hashtag, the online community simply changed to a new iteration of the tag. #YaMeCanse went through 34 iterations to avoid being destroyed by Peñabots. Of the 34 iterations, 23 made it into the trending bar of Twitter.[62]

This failure of Peñabots to disrupt this message highlights the ability of dedicated human users to innovate around bots. Disaffected Twitter users were able to limit the impact of the Peñabots by recognizing their presence and adapting their hashtag strategy to outwit the bots. Their strategy was easy to understand for users (if a hashtag is compromised, try the same hashtag but add the next number) but challenging for the bots to combat. In essence, political fervor and human

---

[58] Gabriela Torres, Charlotte McDonald, and Anne-Marke Tomchak, "#BBCTtrending: 'I Am Tired': The Politics of Mexico's #Yamecanse Hashtag," BBC, December 9, 2014.

[59] Pablo Suárez-Serrato et al., "On the Influence of Social Bots in Online Protests," *Proceedings of the 8th International Conference on Social Informatics, Part II, LNCS*, Vol. 10047, 2016.

[60] Andrea Gompf, "Was the #Yamecansé Hashtag Hijacked by EPN Twitter Bots?" *Remezcla*, 2014.

[61] Gompf, 2014.

[62] Gallagher, 2015.

dexterity outweighed the strength of the bots. As one individual tweeted using the #YaMeCanse2 tag when the first tag was spammed: "#YaMeCanse2 Es TT Mundial ! Así de fuerte es la indignación de todo #México contra @EPN ! Esto ya no lo para Nadie !!!" Translated, the message reads: "It's a trending topic worldwide! This is how strong the indignation is with @EPN [Enrique Peña Nieto]! Nobody can stop this anymore!"

Takeaways

As the cases examined above show, bots can be used in a variety of ways to change SM dynamics, whether by interacting with an individual on a personal level or by working together to alter the larger SM landscape. Their image, influence, and mobilization, whether as a single bot or a network, all play a role in their ability to affect and influence human users. Bots can empower humans, connecting and assisting them in scalable ways.

However, these cases highlight the importance of paying careful attention to the context in which bots are deployed, as practical tactical choices can empower or hamper bot operations. First, platforms, cultures, and governmental regimes affect engagement structures, styles, and expectations. Second, image constrains or expands the impact of a given account; profiles that already appear to be influential via high follower or friend counts and that appear to belong to the in-group of the intended target are more likely to be taken seriously. Lastly, network connections matter. Bots with mutual friends with a target are more likely to be friended, and users with high friend counts are less likely to scrutinize bots. Preexisting communities of densely connected users may be more difficult to infiltrate than target users connected only loosely by common interest in a particular topic. The higher profile achieved by more active bot networks means both wider influence and higher likelihood of detection and suspension.

Even with all these factors working in harmony, bots do not constitute a silver bullet. Creative opponents adapt to static bot tactics, limiting the effectiveness of operations, especially those that try to disrupt networks. Bots will only be as effective as the code and algorithms that underlie them and direct their actions. To that end, we next turn to the question of the maturity of bot technology.

Maturity Model

Bot technology is still rapidly developing, but most bot components have advanced to a point where the deployment of bots appears viable, at least for certain purposes. Bot technology is far from monolithic; a bot's success will depend on how many and which functions that bot is asked to perform and generally on an interrelated set of tasks. For purposes of fashioning a maturity model, we divide these many technical functions into three primary categories: sense, decide, and act. For each function, drawing on our literature reviews, case studies, and SME interviews, we assess the maturity of the related technology as mature, current, or further. "Mature" refers to well-developed capabilities. "Current" means capabilities that, as of 2017, are developed enough to be of some practical use and can expect significant improvements in the future. "Further" is defined as capabilities that are significantly farther away in development, though they are reasonably expected to be available in the more-distant future.

Sense

"Sense" functions involve the ability to find, store, and "make sense," at a low concept level, of content in an automated fashion and are presented in Table 2.1.

The sense capabilities of bots are generally well developed enough to be of real practical use. However, substantial future developments appear likely, particularly in the realm of using natural language processing (NLP) to improve automated understanding of human speech patterns. Being able to distinguish subtle shades of meaning—such as sarcasm—still eludes bots, particularly within languages other than English.

Decide

"Decide" functions essentially refer to the capacity to sort content or other data into meaningful buckets, enabling decisions to be made about each piece of content or user in an automated fashion, and are presented in Table 2.2.

Table 2.1
Sensing Capabilities

Capability	Description	Maturity
Text capture	Ability to detect and store text on SM platforms	Mature
Image capture	Detect and store images shared on SM platforms	Mature
Video/sound capture	Detect and store video and audio shared on SM platforms	Mature
Process text	Natural language processing (NLP) capacity to interpret hashtags, keywords, and phrases	Current
Speech to text	NLP capacity to convert spoken conversational language to text (e.g., Siri)	Current
Machine translation	NLP capacity to translate from one language to another	Current
Demographic targeting	Look for particular demographics, either by platform selection or within some platforms (e.g., real-time bidding technologies)	Current

Table 2.2
Deciding Capabilities

Capability	Description	Maturity
Classify text	Machine-based capacity to classify text at scale (e.g., classify tweets as pro- or anti-ISIL)	Mature
Classify images	Machine-based capacity to classify images at scale	Current
Classify video	Machine-based capacity to classify video at scale (e.g., recruitment videos, execution videos)	Current
Detect/map networks	Autonomously identify and map networks	Current
Triage	Classify at the level of interaction (e.g., recruitment, request for help)	Current
Semiautomated bot detection	Ability to differentiate between a human user and a bot with human supervision and occasional inputs	Current
Automated bot detection	Ability to differentiate between a human user and a bot automatically and without human training	Current/ further (arms race)

Bot decisionmaking abilities are also well developed enough to be useful. However, machine error still persists at varying levels; the graver the consequences of misclassification, the more caution should be applied when trusting bots to engage in autonomous decisionmaking.

The arms race between the ability of humans to detect bots, or the ability to perform automated or semiautomated bot detection, and the ability of bots to evade such detection was a key insight brought up repeatedly by SMEs in interviews.[63] Multiple interviewees thought that as of 2017, the edge rested with bot detectors.[64] One representative of an SM management tool company reported that after it instituted a sign-up filter to prevent ISIL from signing up droves of bot accounts, someone emailed the company's chief security officer and offered him a six-figure dollar amount to "let them continue making accounts."[65] However, the chief security officer reported that the company was employing ML so that it could detect future patterns as they grew more complex. Interviewees emphasized that the advantage between bot detection and evasion was likely to switch back and forth as each side surged forward with new developments, prompting the other to innovate around the advances. For instance, as future bots expand into multimedia, potentially automatically generating images and video, a new suite of detection tools will be required.[66]

Act

"Act" functions involve the ability to take some virtual or real-world action, such as tweeting, sending a friend request, or replying to a comment, in an automated fashion, following a decision about how to act.

---

63 Interview with academic expert with military cyber background, November 22, 2016; interview with academic expert with a DoD tech background, November 16, 2016; and interview with tech industry expert who liaises with USG clients and previously worked at DoD, December 15, 2016.

64 Interview with academic expert with a DoD tech background, November 16, 2016; interview with tech industry expert who liaises with USG clients and previously worked at DoD, December 15, 2016.

65 Interview with SM management tool provider, November 8, 2016.

66 Interview with academic expert with a DoD tech background, November 16, 2016.

The preceding "decision" about what action to take may be a result of human-coded rules, the automated output of a DL algorithm, or any of the "decide" functions discussed in the above section. Action capabilities are presented in Table 2.3.

Bot technology is sufficiently advanced to take action in a variety of ways, particularly those involving one-way messaging rather than two-way sustained interaction. Tweeting to a hashtag channel, liking or retweeting the posts of other users, and sending one-off messages or a deluge of obviously repetitive messages to a given user are all well within bot capabilities as of 2017. However, bots are generally not yet able to hold sustained conversations with human users without raising the suspicion that they are automatons. When careful listening and intelligent responses are needed, particularly in critical situations, handing a user over to a human-in-the-loop or matchmaking a user with a human helper may be necessary.

The next generation of bots will threaten to move beyond text generation to audio and video manipulation, not only opening up the

Table 2.3
Action Capabilities

Capability	Description	Maturity
Broadcast	Post information (text, videos, links)	Mature
Engage	Respond with targeted, relevant information (text, videos, links)	Current
Repeat/amplify	Repeat or reshare another account's content	Current
Harass	Target someone on SM with hostile or threatening language	Current
Matchmake	Match two people—generally someone in need of assistance with human responders who can help (e.g., a young person thinking about fighting abroad being matched with a former fighter)	Current
Response tree	Follow a conversational tree to inform bot response logic	Current
Converse	Fluently use natural language in human or humanlike ways, generally by relying on AI and ML	Further
Synthesize	Generate audio or video along a certain theme	Further

world of video- and audio-based SM to bot participation but also constituting a powerful weapon for disinformation that can be used and abused by allies and adversaries alike. While this technology is not yet widely or commercially available, researchers at the University of Washington have already demonstrated the ability to synthesize video to effectively put new words in a person's mouth.[67]

Conclusions

Broadly speaking, bot technology can be assessed as somewhere in the middle of its development life cycle, with advances both ongoing and likely to occur in the near future. Major technological hurdles have been overcome, but the technology has a long way to go before exhausting its suggested potential. For the purposes of bot operations, technology has developed enough that bots can successfully perform many desired functions, enabling the varied successes exhibited by the foregoing case studies.

These case studies show how bots have been employed for a wide variety of purposes on SM, from triaging health concerns and enabling peer emotional support to broadcasting political messages, disrupting opponent activities, and harvesting intelligence. Bots that interact with humans one-on-one, as well as vast networks of bots that target whole communities, can empower humans in scalable ways but can also be outmaneuvered by dedicated and intelligent human opponents. The various outcomes of these efforts highlight the importance of paying careful attention to various practical and nontechnological factors, including the platforms, cultures, and governmental regimes in which a bot is deployed; the profile characteristics of the social bot, including apparent social influence and group identity; the activity level of the bot and its methods of content generation; and the network characteristics of users that a bot is attempting to befriend or influence.

However, beyond the technological questions about bot development and the practical questions about bot deployment tactics, another

---

[67] Suwajanakorn, Seitz, and Kemelmacher-Shlizerman, 2017.

set of factors merits serious consideration: legal and ethical implications. As an evolving arena that spans borders and jurisdictions, SM has become a vital and highly charged platform for political discourse. Any deployment of bots by government actors must be constrained by these considerations. Accordingly, Chapter Three examines bot programs from a legal and ethical perspective.

CHAPTER THREE

Potential Legal and Ethical Risks

This chapter addresses some of the legal and ethical risks associated with USG use of bots for counterterrorism (CT) or other purposes. It does not constitute a legal review but rather a policy-oriented overview of the considerations the USG should take into account when deciding whether and how to use bots in online countermessaging or CT efforts. The chapter has divided the considerations along legal and ethical lines; however, this is not intended to draw a sharp distinction between these considerations. Some of the ethical considerations might have legal analogs, whereas legal considerations often give rise to or stem from ethical risks. General principles of legal and ethical risk, as well as possible risk mitigations, are summarized here.

First, risks vary by bot type, target, deployer, and objective.

Second, bot programs, even if used exclusively domestically, have international consequences. The USG may set precedents that normalize other states' actions. Bots that interfere with the confidentiality, integrity, or availability of information might be seen as threatening cybersecurity. We acknowledge, however, that there is no guarantee that any given USG action will become normative.

Third, there are risks involved with information collected through bot programs, and the USG may mitigate risk through established mechanisms for information collection and privacy protection.

Fourth, the USG cannot use a bot to conduct actions that would be prohibited if done without the bot. Thus, the USG cannot promote false messages and use bots assuming false identities in "human" disguises. Public articulation of principles for how the USG will deploy bots may mitigate risk.

Fifth, partnering with internet platforms in the private sector will alleviate some ethical risk. This includes the USG carefully considering whether bots comply with the ToS agreements of internet and SM platforms as well as seeking permission from internet platforms before bot deployment. Finally, the USG would face serious risk and scrutiny should it try to pressure or coerce internet platforms to remove protected content.

Legal Considerations

Legal considerations examined in this section include First Amendment protections, implications for law enforcement and intelligence collection, Smith-Mundt Act restrictions on propaganda, material support to terrorism provisions, and international laws and norms in cyberspace.

First Amendment Considerations

Free Speech Clause

The Free Speech Clause of the First Amendment protects broad categories of speech from government regulation, including speech conducted online using internet platforms. This robust protection extends to an expansive variety of content, including speech of a political nature. Not all speech is protected, and nonprotected speech includes content that incites violence or provides material support to designated terrorist groups.[1] However, the line distinguishing protected from nonprotected speech is not always sharp when it comes to the varieties of terrorist material posted online.[2] For instance, some forms of speech potentially associated with terrorism, such as circulating ISIL news bulletins or

---

1 *Brandenburg v. Ohio*, 315 U.S. 568 (1969); *Chaplinsky v. New Hampshire*, 315 U.S. 568 (1942); U.S. Code Title 18, Section 2339A, Providing Material Support to Terrorists, November 2, 2002.

2 Interview with two legal scholars focused on digital threats to civil society, December 19, 2016; interview with government official 2, March 6, 2017.

posting beheading videos, might be considered political speech protected from government regulation.[3]

If specific internet content is protected, the USG is constitutionally prohibited from restricting or regulating that content unless strict scrutiny and other high legal standards are met. In seeking to remove content or block users, the USG is required to follow established legal procedures, such as securing court orders.[4] If bots are deployed by the government to remove content, then by this principle, they should also follow established legal procedures.

In addition to the prohibitions on regulating protected speech, the USG faces questions concerning the legal permissibility of engaging with internet platforms regarding their policies toward online content. Internet platforms such as Twitter and Facebook require users to comply with ToS agreements that frequently include prohibitions on circulating terrorist propaganda or beheading videos, even if that content would be considered protected from government regulation. These platforms regularly permit and even encourage users to flag content that potentially violates their ToS for review and possible removal or account suspension. To coordinate and formalize mechanisms to flag potential ToS violations, the UK government set up a Counter Terrorism Referral Unit, which reportedly removes 2,000 pieces of extremist material per week.[5] Similarly, the European Union established the Internet Referral Unit in 2015, which in its first year processed over 11,000 messages.[6]

[3] Jaclyn Haughom, "Combatting Terrorism in a Digital Age: First Amendment Implications," *Freedom Forum Institute*, November 16, 2016; interview with two legal scholars focused on digital threats to civil society, December 19, 2016.

[4] For example, *Zablocki v. Redhail*, 434 U.S. 374 (1978); *Reno v. ACLU*, 96 U.S. 511 (1997).

[5] National Police Chiefs' Council, "The Counter Terrorism Internet Referral Unit," website, undated; "250,000th Piece of Online Extremist/Terrorist Material to Be Removed," Metropolitan Police, 2016.

[6] Europol, "Europol Internet Referral Unit One Year On," press release, The Hague, The Netherlands, July 22, 2016.

The USG has considered whether to establish a similar centralized content-flagging mechanism.[7] However, there may be legal questions about the permissibility of the USG establishing such a mechanism, and First Amendment considerations will have to guide the shape it should take. It is one thing for everyday users to flag potential ToS violations but another thing if the USG, perhaps with an implicit or perceived threat of coercion, does the flagging. Government lawyers will need to review the limits on the USG's ability to flag content that might be a ToS violation but is nevertheless protected by the First Amendment. If a bot is deployed to flag potential ToS violations, the details of how the bot interfaces with the internet platforms will matter, in particular whether it might be imposing constitutionally prohibited undue influence on internet platforms.

Establishment Clause

The Establishment Clause of the First Amendment holds that the USG is prohibited from actions that unduly favor one religion over another.[8] Depending on details of a given government-run bot program, this clause may present legal questions for bot types that target users on the basis of their religion or have a disparate impact on a specific religious group. Bot types that might be susceptible to this risk include influence, harvest, matchmaker, masquerade, and harassment bots. Legal questions will hinge on whether designing or deploying bots that target users on religious grounds—for instance, by employing religion-specific keywords—and that include American citizens in the intended or incidental target audience constitute actions that unduly disfavor the religion.

A possible mitigation for this legal barrier is to focus on engaging targeted communities abroad that are unlikely to include Americans and that are not targeted on the basis of religion. According to former Global Engagement Center (GEC) director Michael Lumpkin, the GEC has already conducted "scalpel messaging" campaigns that consist of "highly targeted messages that go to the most vulnerable

---

[7] Interview with government official 2, March 6, 2017.

[8] For summary, see Cornell University, "Establishment Clause," webpage, Legal Information Institute, Cornell University Law School, undated.

audiences."[9] A narrowly targeted approach for bot deployment abroad may alleviate potential Establishment Clause concerns. Bot developers should also think carefully about the keywords they will use to target users to ensure that they are not overbroad or narrowly religion-based, and that they will not be directed at Americans.

Law Enforcement and Intelligence

Some bot types, including harvest bots, have potential benefits for law enforcement or intelligence efforts. However, if these bots are deployed for law enforcement purposes or to collect information on targets that goes beyond publicly available data, they are subject to specific legal constraints and processes. The details on what type of bot is involved and how it collects information will matter when determining which laws are applicable. Relevant law and directives include but are not limited to the Privacy Act, the Electronic Communications Privacy Act, the Communication Assistance to Law Enforcement Act, the Stored Communications Act, the Foreign Intelligence Surveillance Act, and Executive Order 12333.

Before a bot is deployed for law enforcement or information collection, the agency deploying the bot will need to ensure it has the appropriate authority to conduct that mission. For instance, if the bot is deployed by an agency such as the State Department, and the bot goes beyond public data mining to engage users for information-gathering purposes, the agency will need to identify the legal constraints and processes for protecting the information and potentially sharing it with law enforcement or intelligence agencies.

Although not strictly speaking a legal issue, a related ethical question concerns the permissibility of sharing information harvested by bots with international partners. Many CT partners have fewer human rights and privacy protections, and the USG should carefully consider the consequences of sharing collected information with them.[10]

---

[9] Joby Warrick, "How a U.S. Team Uses Facebook, Guerilla Marketing to Peel Off Potential ISIS Recruits," *Washington Post*, February 6, 2017.

[10] Freedom House, *Freedom of the Net 2016—Silencing the Messenger: Communication Apps Under Pressure*, Washington, D.C.: Freedom House, November 2016; interview with two online CVE intervention program directors, December 20, 2016.

These considerations can be mitigated by developing and deploying bots for purely countermessaging goals, rather than by using harvest-type bots for law enforcement or intelligence.[11] Agencies such as the State Department can also consider establishing firewalls between its bot deployment and law enforcement agencies. Insofar as bots are deployed for law enforcement or intelligence purposes, all relevant statutes and processes should be followed. In particular, if the bot collects personally identifiable information (PII) of Americans, then the agency needs to protect privacy as codified in relevant law.

Smith-Mundt Act

The United States Information and Education Exchange Act of 1948, more commonly known as the Smith-Mundt Act, enables the State Department and the Broadcasting Board of Governors (BBG) to conduct public diplomacy campaigns abroad but restricts their ability "to influence public opinion in the United States."[12] This law reflects long-standing concerns about USG-generated—and taxpayer-funded—domestic propaganda, and it seeks to limit the dissemination of government-produced material to U.S. audiences. The Smith-Mundt Modernization Act of 2012 updated the law to permit the State Department and the BBG to make information intended for foreign audiences available to the U.S. domestic population.[13] However, prohibitions on the USG creating content that is intended for audiences in the United States remain in effect.

The Smith-Mundt Act introduces legal constraints on how State Department bot operations might be conducted. The State Department will need to carefully review the act to ensure that any deployed bots satisfy domestic exposure restrictions. State lawyers will also need to carefully consider what constitutes an "audience" with regard to bots to ensure that intended audiences are foreign persons.

---

[11] Interview with two online CVE intervention program directors, December 20, 2016.

[12] U.S. Code Title 22, Section 1431, United States Information and Educational Exchange Act of 1948 (Smith-Mundt Act), January 27, 1948.

[13] Included in Section 1078 of Public Law 112–239, National Defense Authorization Act for Fiscal Year 2013, January 2, 2013.

The legal restrictions associated with the Smith-Mundt Act, like the Establishment Clause consideration discussed above, suggest that the USG and the State Department in particular should ensure that bots are carefully programmed to target messaging at specific foreign audiences.

Material Support Provisions

Title 18 of the U.S. Code (which includes provisions from the USA PATRIOT Act) prohibits the delivery of material support to designated terrorist groups. Material support comprises four types of activities: "training," "expert advice or assistance," "service," and "personnel."[14] U.S. courts have defended the law against legal challenges and have issued rulings that further clarify the scope of the prohibition. Notably, in *Holder v. Humanitarian Law Project*, the Supreme Court ruled that assistance that was intended to help two designated terrorist groups peacefully resolve conflict—in particular, the Kurdistan Worker's Party and the Liberation Tigers of Tamil Eelam—constituted a "service" that legitimized the groups and was thus prohibited material support.[15]

This ruling raises questions about bot operations, especially with respect to any bot that interacts with members of a designated terrorist group.[16] For instance, would deploying an influence bot intended to persuade ISIL members to defect constitute material support? What if the target is only further radicalized and goes on to commit a terrorist act—would that then constitute material support?

Agencies considering deploying bots will need to closely assess how material support prohibitions are interpreted in courts. They should carefully program and deploy bots to ensure they are not engaging with designated terrorists in such a way that could be interpreted as providing training, expert advice or assistance, service, or personnel. For instance, rather than targeting bots at active ISIL members, bots could be targeted to engage with at-risk populations that are not yet associated with a terrorist group.

---

[14] U.S. Code Title 18, Section 2339A(b), 2002.

[15] *Holder v. Humanitarian Law Project*, 561 U.S. 1 (2010).

[16] Interview with two online CVE intervention program directors, December 20, 2016.

Additional Legal Uncertainty

As an emergent technology, bots would constitute a relatively novel tool for CT and CVE efforts, and a number of legal uncertainties remain. This chapter has sought to identify some of the major legal considerations that apply to bots, but other legal principles might also be applicable. Below are some additional questions regarding bots that might require further legal analysis.

Entrapment: The USG is prohibited from actions that "originate a criminal design, implant in an innocent person's mind the disposition to commit a criminal act, and then induce commission of the crime."[17] As one SME observed, the USG will need to be careful that its bot deployment cannot be construed as "entrapping" its targets by inducing them to commit acts of terrorism.[18] Here the details of bot deployment will matter, and bot developers will need to monitor and guard against this legal uncertainty.

Even basic questions such as who bears legal responsibility for a bot's actions are still being determined. In Switzerland, artists Carmen Weisskopf and Domagoj Smoljom designed an automated online shopping bot to buy random items from the deep web for an art exhibit; when the bot purchased ten ecstasy pills in January 2014, a local prosecutor seized the exhibition. However, the illegal drugs were later returned to the creators because they successfully argued that the exhibit was art in the public interest.[19]

Enabling partners: The USG may consider partnering with private sector or nongovernmental organizations (NGOs) to deploy bots. This leads to the question of whether working with enabling partners to run bot programs (as opposed to the USG's running them) will alleviate legal and ethical concerns. However, according to one legal expert from a U.S. civil society organization, "government cannot outsource what it

---

[17] *Jacobson v. United States*, 503 U.S. 540 (1992).

[18] Interview with two online CVE intervention program directors, December 20, 2016.

[19] Mike Power, "What Happens When a Software Bot Goes on a Darknet Shopping Spree?" *The Guardian*, December 5, 2014; Katie Grant, "Random Darknet Shopper: Exhibition Featuring Automated Dark Web Purchases Opens in London," *The Independent*, December 12, 2015.

cannot do."[20] Given that, the United States should be prepared to face the same legal constraints in its partnerships as it faces in its own efforts.

A related question regarding partnering with outside international actors to deploy bots concerns export controls and the possibility of requiring a license to export bot technology or services. Several export control lists might have applicability to bots, and the USG will need to carefully review which controls apply.

In general, the legal constraints and permissions regarding working with enabling partners require further analysis and review by government lawyers.

International Law and Norms in Cyberspace

In addition to domestic law, USG bot developers and operators should also consider international legal and ethical considerations. There is a developing global consensus that international law applies to state behavior in cyberspace, but it is still largely unsettled on how international law applies to state actions.[21] The USG has led international discussions on developing international cyber norms; however, efforts to shape an international shared understanding of how states ought to behave in the cyber realm remain immature.

The USG's leadership role on cyber issues prompts difficult ethical questions with respect to bot operations. In developing and deploying bots, the USG should be cognizant of its primary role as a norm setter with respect to state behavior in cyberspace and be prepared for others to follow the U.S. lead or otherwise point to U.S. precedent to justify their own actions. As one SME put it, "What we do online will be modeled by others"—and other countries might not deploy bots as carefully as the USG.[22] To take one case as an example, the United

---

[20] Interview with legal scholar focused on cybersecurity, November 22, 2016.

[21] The applicability of international law to cyberspace was affirmed by the leaders of the G20 in 2015. G20, "G20 Leaders' Communiqué," Antalya Summit, Turkey, November 16, 2015. For one description of the unsettled nature of international law, see Department of Defense Law of War Manual, Office of General Counsel Department of Defense, June 12, 2015.

[22] Interview with government official 1, March 6, 2017.

States is a signatory and global champion of the International Covenant on Civil and Political Rights (ICCPR), in which several articles have potential relevance to bots. In particular, Article 2 requires that parties respect human rights without regard for religion, and Article 19 protects freedom of expression.[23] Although as a legal matter the United States does not view the ICCPR as applying extraterritorially to noncitizens, as a policy matter the United States has sought to promote these principles for all persons and has criticized other countries for not abiding by their ICCPR commitments. One SME expressed concern that if U.S. actions are perceived as violating the principles or even the spirit of the ICCPR protections, then the United States will lose its ability to hold other countries accountable or, at the very least, will face severe charges of hypocrisy.[24]

In addition, specific types of bots might raise particular international objections and have other diplomatic ramifications. In particular, the USG should be wary of bots that would be likely to be perceived as violating the sovereignty of other countries or otherwise threatening global cybersecurity. Cybersecurity is regularly defined as the effort to promote the confidentiality, integrity, or availability of data. This definition is used widely both by the USG (for example, within the Federal Information Security Management Act)[25] and in multilateral venues (for example, within the Organisation for Economic Co-operation and Development).[26] USG actions that put confidentiality, integrity, or availability of data at risk might be seen as an aggressive cyber operation that threatens cybersecurity. Some bot activities seem to interfere with the availability and integrity of information—for instance, bots that redirect users to preferred content, bots that alter content, or bots that disrupt users' ability to access content. Bots that create

---

[23] United Nations, International Covenant on Civil and Political Rights, New York, December 16, 1966.

[24] Interview with government official 1, March 6, 2017.

[25] U.S. Code, Title 44, Section 3541, Federal Information Security Management Act of 2002, December 17, 2002.

[26] OECD, *OECD Guidelines for the Security of Information Systems, 1992*, Paris, France: OECD, 2002.

smokescreens or drown out opponents with noise might also be seen as threatening the availability or integrity of information. In general, the United States should carefully consider whether these activities would potentially be perceived as undermining global cybersecurity.

Ethical Considerations

As previously noted, the legal and ethical considerations that apply at a general level to bot operations cannot be sharply distinguished from each other, and several ethical considerations have already been mentioned. However, a variety of advocates, organizations, and SMEs have raised an additional set of ethical considerations they deem to be relevant when considering bot design and deployment.

Industry Impact

In conducting bot operations, the USG leverages privately owned internet platforms to achieve CT and CVE objectives. The internet and SM platforms themselves have their own interests and business goals, and the USG should be aware of these interests when it seeks to use privately owned and operated services. In particular, many internet companies have indicated the importance of preserving the liability protections over user-generated content provided by section 230 of the Communication Decency Act.[27] Recent cases such as *Fields v. Twitter* have raised the question of how platforms and providers navigate the tension between trying to prevent their platforms from being used for nefarious purposes and not putting themselves in the position of being liable for content on their sites by exercising editorial control. The use of bots by the USG might further complicate the platforms' ability to maintain this neutrality if the platforms are pressured to support USG bot programs or are otherwise perceived to give editorial preference to USG-deployed bots.

In addition, as previously noted, internet platforms have widely varying ToS agreements, including specific permissions and prohibi-

---

[27] Interview with legal scholar focused on cybersecurity, November 22, 2016.

tions with respect to the deployment of bots. For example, Twitter prohibits bots that conduct hashtag spamming (which might include prohibition of dis/information and noise bots). Telegram's restrictions are more limited, but do require bots to self-identify as bots.[28] Table 3.1 summarizes example ToS agreements.

The USG has promoted the use of the internet as a driver of social and economic growth, and thus it should consider steps that will help alleviate potential risks to companies.[29] For instance, it should carefully review each company's ToS agreement before deploying bots. If the USG continues to encourage or assist companies to actively and effectively remove ToS violations, then it should be especially conscientious that its own use of bots does not itself constitute a violation. In addition, the USG can also consider whether it should seek permission from internet platforms before bots are deployed. By seeking permission, this will ensure that the bots remain within companies' ToS and general level of comfort. Developing partnerships with companies will also likely provide the government insight on how the platforms are used, potentially resulting in more effective bot operations.

Transparency

Several sets of interviews suggested that there is an ethical and practical requirement to be transparent in bot deployment. As one SME put it: "I think an interesting ethical and transparency baseline is for bots to own up to the fact that they are bots. You are on more complicated grounds with bots that act as other actors."[30] Many Americans, and even foreign nationals, have strong cultural expectations that the USG will be honest and direct in its dealings and will generally avoid presenting material that looks like propaganda. As one interviewee stated, "There is a reason we [Americans] are bad at [information operations], because we have a cultural hang-up about government manipulating

---

[28] Nathalie Marechal, "When Bots Tweet: Toward a Normative Framework for Bots on Social Networking Sites," *International Journal of Communication*, Vol. 10, 2016.

[29] Office of the President of the United States, *International Strategy for Cyberspace: Prosperity, Security, and Openness*, Washington, D.C., May 2011.

[30] Interview with tech industry expert, December 15, 2016.

Table 3.1
Terms of Service for Select Social Media Platforms or Messaging Services

Company	Summary of Terms of Service Agreements Regarding Bots
Twitter	• Bots are permitted. • Bots are subject to content restrictions (including restrictions related to trademark, copyright, and graphic content). • Bots cannot be used for spamming (such as automatically posting about trending topics or duplicating tweets on one or multiple accounts), posting misleading links or links that redirect to other pages before final content, engaging in abusive behavior, sharing private information, automated likes, or automated following/unfollowing. • Multiple accounts per user are allowed, although verified accounts follow different rules.
Facebook	• Bots are permitted. • Bots are subject to rules, including that they cannot contact persons in Messenger without their consent and cannot be used for advertising or promotional content without permission. All users, presumably including bots, are prohibited from providing false personal information or creating an account for anyone other than oneself.
Telegram	• Bots are permitted. • Bots are required to be labeled "bot," and they cannot initiate conversations with users.
Reddit	• No specific rules for bots. • However, all users are subject to content restrictions (including bans on spam-like behavior such as flooding a community with content, manual or automated voter manipulation, incitement of violence, threatening or illegal content, or impersonations of someone else "in a misleading or deceptive manner"). • All users are prohibited from "creating multiple accounts to evade punishment or avoid restrictions."
Kik	• Bots are permitted. • Bots are identified as such by an icon attached to their profile picture. • Users are subject to content restrictions (including bans on false, illegal, threatening, graphic, and violent content or content that promotes discrimination) and banned from impersonating other people or entities or spamming Kik users, apparently in the context of soliciting purchases. • Using harvest bots to collect information on other users is not permitted. • Users are not allowed to create a second account if Kik has disabled their first account.

SOURCE: RAND Review of Companies' Terms of Service as follows: Twitter, "Automation Rules," Twitter Help Center, April 6, 2017; Twitter, "The Twitter Rules," Twitter Help Center, undated b; Facebook, "Facebook Platform Policy," Facebook for Developers, undated; Telegram, "Bots: An Introduction for Developers," webpage, undated; Reddit, "Reddit Content Policy," webpage, undated; Kik, "Terms of Service," webpage, February 1, 2017.

information for political ends."[31] The use of bots, especially those that circulate false or misleading information or that deceive users into thinking they are human, cuts against these cultural expectations and could have long-term impacts on how the USG communicates to the world. In addition, deploying bots that are perceived to be dishonest could result in the internet becoming a less-trusted space overall. This development would have economic, commercial, and human rights implications and would set back U.S. policy to promote an open and interoperable internet. Bots that claim to be human, even if they are well designed and highly and technologically sophisticated, are at risk of eventual exposure through technical or other means.

To mitigate these concerns, the USG can consider steps that make its bot operations more transparent. Consider the rough spectrum illustrated in Figure 3.1 of ways in which a bot could be more transparent or less transparent.

From many advocates' perspectives, the more transparent the bot, the less likely the USG will be perceived to be a dishonest or irresponsible online actor. However, the USG might have specific goals that make more transparency too operationally risky or otherwise unpalatable. One approach is that for each bot it deploys, the government can assess the highest level of transparency it can maintain while still accomplishing the bot's goals.

Another approach to guard against the perception of mistrust is for the USG to produce a statement of public principles describing at a high level the types of bots the USG will deploy and the ways it will

Figure 3.1
Transparency Spectrum

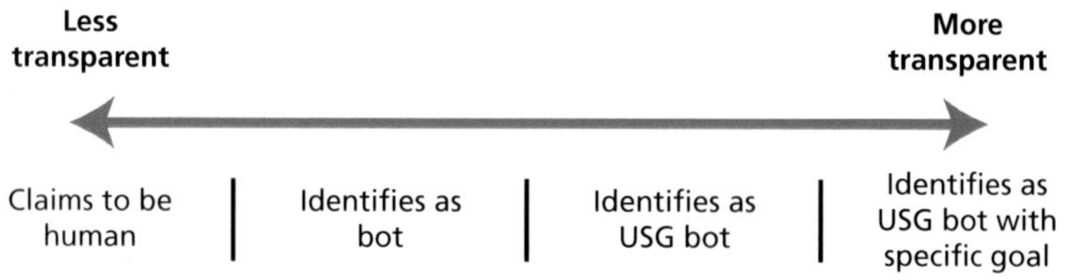

[31] Interview with legal scholar focused on cybersecurity, November 22, 2016.

deploy them. A statement of principles would enable the public to have a better understanding of what the United States is doing with bots and the limits of its bot operations. It would also help codify and establish norms of responsible bot usage and distinguish USG usage from the ways other governments or users use bots for malicious purposes. The USG could even consider partnering with internet platforms to craft this statement of principles, thereby bolstering these important partnerships.

Differing Agencies and Objectives

A variety of USG agencies participate in CT and CVE missions and might seek to leverage bots for their operations. Several SMEs argued that certain agencies incur greater ethical risks by using bots than others.[32] In particular, the State Department's mission is very broad and contains objectives beyond CT and CVE, including consular affairs, promoting U.S. economic interests, and promoting internet freedom and human rights around the world. This potentially involves risks that State Department–deployed bots might create collateral effects or a perception that could undermine State's other missions. On the other hand, agencies without the consular missions or that are directly involved in the promotion of internet freedom—such as the Department of Homeland Security—might be better positioned to develop and deploy bots without the same type of direct collateral impact.

Slippery Intervention Slope

From the perspective of both consumer trust and privacy, platforms, tech companies, and internet users worry about the slippery slope of government intervention into the relatively unregulated space of the internet. The internet has developed partly because of the dynamic and innovative nature of the private sector and partly because it has been viewed as a place where users can freely associate and express themselves without fear of government crackdown. As noted above, the line between protected political speech and "illegal" terrorist material is not always sharp, and internet platforms have found themselves in a deli-

---

[32] Interview with government official 1, March 6, 2017.

cate balance. Several legal scholars interviewed for this report voiced concern that the use of bots might create a chilling effect on free speech and that users will be hesitant to express themselves if they believe they are being monitored.[33]

Chapter Four delves further into risks and benefit trade-offs for specific components of bot operations in the effort to operationalize some of the insights from this legal and ethical review.

---

[33] Interview with two legal scholars focused on digital threats to civil society, December 19, 2016.

CHAPTER FOUR

Concepts of Operation and Assessment

We have concluded that bots are a potentially plausible and effective means of conducting CT or CVE interventions against groups like ISIL. The logical next step for the USG is the development and implementation of specific bot programs to combat ISIL and similar threats. An intermediate step is to assess and choose between different concepts of operations (CONOPs). By CONOPs, we mean general approaches for programs. For example, a program that tries to proactively offer resources and support to populations at risk for radicalization is very different from a bot program aimed at combating misinformation spread by U.S. adversaries.

To help evaluate and choose between different CONOPs, we offer criteria for assessing CONOPs, incorporating technical feasibility, risks to SM users, risks to bot deployers, potential impact, and complexity. We then deconstruct bots (CONOPs) into component parts, which we call variables; these include factors such as target audience, attribution level, automation, and platform. Next, we apply our assessment criteria (described in detail below) to several levels at which these variables could be set in given concepts of operation; for instance, we assess the technical feasibility of the communication strategy of narrowcasting to a specific audience. Lastly, we articulate concepts of action for 12 types of bots and consider the risk and benefit trade-offs associated with each potential platform. The intent is not to provide a definitive judgment on what the "best" bot program would look like but rather to design a comprehensive method of assessing different combinations of bot program components.

However, some relative judgments can be made. In the category of bots that seek to influence and inform target audiences, matchmaker and prompter bots appear the most feasible in terms of available technology and risk. Among bots that attempt to degrade or disrupt extremist networks, an exposer bot seems to be the most immediately practicable since it combines technical feasibility with relatively low risk for both the builder and general populations of SM users. As for bots that collect intelligence, harvest bots are more technologically feasible than mousetrap bots. While no conceptual bot program is without risk and no potential impact is guaranteed, a well-informed assessment and conceptualization offers any potential bot program the best chance for success.

Assessment Criteria and Levels

Our assessment framework incorporates the following five criteria for bot operations: (1) technical feasibility, (2) personal risks to SM users, (3) risks to the builders or deployers of bots, (4) the potential impact of the operation in terms of either breadth or depth, and (5) the complexity involved in undertaking the operation. Using this framework, our team synthesized findings from SME interviews, case studies, and our literature review. Based on that synthesis, team members worked out consensus ratings for each component. The following sections unpack the results of this assessment to component variables of bot operations, assessing a number of possible values at which these variables could be set as green (indicating confidence), yellow (representing caution), or orange (signifying extreme caution). These criteria and relative assessment indicators are detailed below in Table 4.1.

Table 4.1
Assessment Levels

Shade	Meaning
	Few limitations or concerns (proceed with relative confidence)
	Considerable limitations or concerns (proceed with caution)
	Serious limitations or concerns (proceed with extreme caution)

Our first assessment criterion, addressing the research or engineering effort to make an operation a reality, is technical feasibility. As an example of the contextual meaning of the above assessment levels, in this context, green signifies well-developed, mature technological capabilities, with few limitations or concerns. Yellow means the relevant technology is advanced enough to be of substantial use, but with potential pitfalls. Orange means the technology required for the operation is beyond or seriously stretches capabilities through 2017.

Second, to account for the privacy, social, and material risks to users who engage with or are engaged by bots, we consider user/personal risks.

Third, to weigh optics risks to the builder or deployer of bots from attribution, perverse effects, and legal challenges, we evaluate builder/deployer risks. In both of these contexts, green relates to minimal risks, yellow means significant risks that need to be weighed carefully, and orange indicates severe and potentially game-ending risks.

Fourth, in order to integrate the magnitude of the projected effect in specific dimensions, such as breadth of reach or quality of interaction, we examine the potential impact. For instance, green could mean broad projected impact or that the predicted impact on a small set of targets is likely to be of a high quality. Yellow could signify a medium score along each of these dimensions, while orange could suggest extremely limited or shallow projected impact.

Lastly, to account for how much coordination, synchronization, and interoperability are required by a given concept of operation, we consider the complexity. In this context, green means relative simplicity or straightforwardness, with fewer actors whose coordination is required for operation success. Yellow indicates more complexity, while orange suggests potentially unworkable levels of required interoperability.

Bot Variables

The following 11 variables are organized according to what type of question about a bot operation they answer: who is involved, where are the bots being deployed, what communication strategy are the bots using, when do the bots act, how do the bots operate, and at what level of visibility is all of this occurring? The specific variable names we have devised are Deployer, Target Audience, Platform Space, Communication Strategy, Activation and Initiation, Automation, Reliance on AI and DL, Data Retention, Volume, "Human" Disguise, and Attribution. Relevant aspects of the assessment criteria defined above are applied to a variety of possible "levels" at which these variables can be set.

There is some variation in which of the five assessment criteria are applied to each specific variable, based on relevance. For instance, technical feasibility applies to variables that deal with what is implemented and how it is implemented, rather than who is implementing the program. Further, some criteria are broken down into two component parts, such as builder risk in the first variable below, to highlight different types of risk to the builder; or potential impact, to distinguish between the breadth of audience affected by the bot program and how deeply or successfully each user reached is affected by that program.

Who?

Two variables are involved in answering the question of who is involved in a bot operation: who is building or deploying the bots, and who is the target audience for the bot activity? Table 4.2 illustrates this assessment.

Table 4.2
Variable Assessment: Deployer

Option	Builder Risk: Control	Builder Risk: Authority Limitations	Potential Impact: Credibility with Target Audience	Complexity
USG				
Partner nation				
NGO/Private sector				

NOTE: The entity deploys the bot. Green = proceed with confidence, yellow = proceed with caution, orange = proceed with extreme caution. Because technical feasibility depends more on what is to be implemented than who deploys the program, it was omitted as a criterion for this variable. Conversely, while one type of risk is increased by designating the USG as the deployer, another type is decreased, so the criteria of builder risk were bifurcated.

Setting the deployer of bots as a USG entity implies more control for the USG as well as less complexity, as fewer parties are involved to complicate interoperability. However, a USG deployer also entails limited authorities, constraining the kind of impact possible without running into legal or ethical issues. Different potential builders within the USG have different authorities and may also have varying levels of credibility or raise varying levels of concern with different target audiences. One interviewee expressed more concern over the FBI operating a bot CVE program due to entrapment and other ethical issues and suggested that an agency like Health and Human Services would engender more trust that the bot program would work to support vulnerable individuals rather than reporting them to law enforcement.[1]

Assisting a partner nation in developing bot capabilities would mean ceding considerable control and could potentially come with its own set of legal constraints, but a partner nation or NGO may have expanded legal authorities.[2] Outsourcing deployment to a non-USG entity would come with increased insulation from reporting requirements to other agencies and the accompanying pressure to exploit information gained on at-risk individuals, alleviating some privacy risks to SM users.[3] One legal scholar we interviewed opined that the key question is what repercussions bots would have for users—that "the mere annoyance of receiving posts" would not pose a major problem, but "more serious repercussions like authorities being alerted, reputational harm, harm to credit score, etc." would raise more privacy and free speech concerns.[4]

Sponsoring an NGO to run a bot program implies not only less control but also more credibility with target audiences and possibly

---

[1] Interview with two online CVE intervention program directors, December 20, 2016.

[2] Interview with legal scholar focused on cybersecurity, November 22, 2016; interview with academic expert with history of advising USG on ISIL Twitter activity, November 7, 2016.

[3] Interview with government expert working on CVE and online radicalization, December 9, 2016.

[4] Interview with two legal scholars focused on digital threats to civil society, December 19, 2016.

more latitude to engage in innovative activities.[5] However, multiple legal experts we interviewed emphasized that government cannot legally perform a "run around the First Amendment."[6] One interviewee said, "As government you can't form an agency relationship with [an] outside party and direct them to do things you can't do yourself."[7] Further, while nonstate actors likely have more credibility with target audiences, for private actors like SM platforms, government partnerships are fraught with fears about users' private information being shared with law enforcement or intelligence agencies.[8] Audience-related variables requiring assessment are summarized in Table 4.3.

Table 4.3
Variable Assessment: Audience

Option	Technical Feasibility	Builder Risk
Universal		
U.S. persons		
Non-U.S. persons		
Adversary accounts (e.g., confirmed ISIL members)		
At risk of radicalization		
Enemy of my enemy (e.g., anti-ISIL activists)		
Adults		
Minors		

NOTE: The population/group the bot is meant to influence. Green = proceed with confidence, yellow = proceed with caution, orange = proceed with extreme caution. While audience selection significantly affects both technical feasibility and builder risk, it does not particularly affect complexity in terms of interoperability. User risk depends on what is done to the audience, and judgments about potential impact would vary too widely based on the aim of the program to make a meaningful general characterization for the variable of audience.

[5] Interview with bot industry expert with IC background, October 20, 2016.

[6] Interview with two legal scholars focused on digital threats to civil society, December 19, 2016.

[7] Interview with legal scholar focused on cybersecurity, November 22, 2016.

[8] Interview with SM platform provider, November 18, 2016.

Any activity that resembles an attempt to sway the opinion of the general U.S. public raises serious concerns of domestic propagandizing, running grave legal and ethical risks. Accordingly, targeting bot operations to a delimited audience seems necessary. Interacting with U.S. persons rather than non-U.S. persons triggers different authorities for different potential builders or deployers of bot programs. Any bot operation that targets U.S. persons is likely to raise privacy concerns. While reasonable precautions can be taken to target non-U.S. persons rather than U.S. persons, a perfect technological solution to this disambiguation problem is likely to remain elusive, given the borderless nature of online interaction.[9]

Public backlash appears less likely for bots that target only confirmed ISIL members.[10] Further, discerning this type of adversary account, technologically speaking, is likely easier[11] than disambiguating U.S. persons from non-U.S. persons. Anti-ISIL activity on SM also comes with a discernible signature, but bot programs intended to influence ISIL opponents may come with more risks for a builder than ISIL supporters, based on the wide range of people who oppose ISIL.

In contrast, targeting SM users at risk of radicalization may prove challenging along two dimensions. In terms of technical feasibility, some interviewees argued that this type of detection is possible.[12] However, academic literature has no perfect answer for how to predict when humans are at risk for radicalization or how SM use may provide those indicators. As one interviewee put it, the traits of people who end up committing acts of terror "can't be generalized in a way that's scientifically valid or in a way that doesn't profile and infringe on First Amendment protected conduct. . . . I don't know how

9 Interview with academic expert with a DoD tech background, November 16, 2016.

10 Interview with government expert working on CVE and online radicalization, December 9, 2016; interview with academic expert with military cyber background, November 22, 2016.

11 Interview with SM management tool provider, November 8, 2016.

12 Interview with academic expert with history of advising USG on ISIL Twitter activity, November 7, 2016; interview with SM management tool provider, November 8, 2016.

you can make a smart bot here without profiling people."[13] In terms of risk, using religious criteria to target individuals for antiradicalization or intelligence-gathering efforts would particularly endanger First Amendment protections.

As another vulnerable population, children and minors would present a very risky target audience for bots. In addition, verifying the age of SM users with certainty is beyond the reach of current (2017) technology, although reasonable technical precautions can be taken.

In summary, a target audience represents a particularly crucial variable for bot programs and is associated with many possible unintended negative consequences. The potential for risk is amplified by the technological difficulty of distinguishing between certain audiences whose targeting triggers different authorities for different actors.

Where?

Aside from the geographic dimension of target audiences, builders of a bot program must ask "where"—and by this we mean on which platform or platforms will the bots be deployed? These platform-type variables are summarized in Table 4.4.

Even within the category of public SM platforms, there is serious variation in terms of implementation affordances and API options, ToS and ToS enforcement, and the type of audience that can be reached using each platform. Aside from variations in target demographics, Facebook's Messenger, Twitter, Telegram, Reddit, Slack, Google's Allo, Kik, and Skype all have different policies regarding bots. For instance, Twitter provides a REST API that suspends accounts for bot-like activity only when they are flagged by users. Facebook lists a host of restrictions on bot activity, including forbidding bots from initiating contact with users without user invitation. Telegram requires bot usernames to end with the word *bot*. On the other end of the spectrum, Reddit has not specified separate use policies for bots versus human users.

[13] Interview with two legal scholars focused on digital threats to civil society, December 19, 2016.

Table 4.4
Variable Assessment: Platform

Option	Technical Feasibility: Implementation Affordances	Builder Risk: ToS, Allowance for Disguise	Builder Risk: ToS, Enforcement Strictness	Potential Impact: Reach
Public				
Private/deep web				
Dark web				

NOTE: Social media platforms that are publicly available, ones that require invitation or are obscured on the deep web, and ones on the (primarily illegal) dark web. Green = proceed with confidence, yellow = proceed with caution, orange = proceed with extreme caution. Different types of builder risks are affected in varying ways by platform selection, resulting in the two builder risk criteria featured above. However, platform selection does not meaningfully affect complexity in terms of program interoperability, and risks to users depend too much on program aims and tactics to be assessed here.

What?

A bot program designer must also ask: what type of communication strategy are the bots using? Communication strategy dimensions are summarized in Table 4.5.

Table 4.5
Variable Assessment: Communication Strategy

Dimension	Option	Technical Feasibility	Builder Risk: Optics	Builder Risk: Control
Breadth	Broadcast			
	Narrowcast			
Directionality	One-way			
	Interactive			

NOTE: Broad approaches for deploying bots: broadcasting for general audiences versus narrowcasting for very targeted audience; and one-way information push versus interactive bots. Green = proceed with confidence, yellow = proceed with caution, orange = proceed with extreme caution. User risks vary too widely based on the aims and tactics of communication to include here, as does potential impact. Complexity, in terms of program interoperability between different actors, does not depend on the breadth or directionality of communication strategy.

In the context of how widely bot programs communicate, bots can either broadcast or narrowcast. Broadcasting means posting on hashtag channels or retweeting content: actions that push content to anyone surfing a given platform. In contrast, narrowcasting means targeting messages to individual SM users, such as replying to a target's tweets. The latter comes with more complications, both in terms of designing and implementing criteria to target individuals in a way that is useful and does not imperil the First Amendment and in terms of how those individuals react. For instance, an individual who feels singled out is more likely to report the account that reached out to him as engaging in ToS-prohibited activity. Provoking individuals to report accounts for ToS violations is one of the key ways for bot accounts to get suspended.[14]

The second dimension of communication strategy involves directionality. A bot that only posts without engaging in conversations with users is relatively simple to construct and operate. A one-way bot bypasses the complex challenge of simulating human behavior for a sustained period of time in a conversation that can take unpredictable turns, based on whatever the conversant user may decide to say. The potential for screenshots of online interactions in which bots are goaded into making inappropriate comments or simply making embarrassing grammar errors underlies the optics risk accompanying the loss of control inherent in interactive communication. However, some types of persuasion will require appropriately targeted, iterated engagement to be successful. As one online CVE program director put it: "Intervention is a long process. [It's] not just about the content of the information you put out on Twitter. There's a lot of relationship building. A lot of it is getting to know the person [and] building trust—it's a very interactive process."[15]

---

[14] Interview with bot industry expert with IC background, October 20, 2016; Boshmaf et al., 2011.

[15] Interview with two online CVE intervention program directors, December 20, 2016.

When?

Bot program designers must also decide when bots will act and therefore how bots will be activated. Such activation choices are summarized in Table 4.6.

This question involves determining whether a bot program will be manually turned "on" during particular moments of crisis or whether it will be operated on an ongoing basis, waiting for platform activity to trigger bot action. Of course, a program can also be turned "on" only to wait for triggers. Manual deployer initiation will maximize control but may limit the reach of potential impact.

The trigger could be audience initiation, when the human user reaches out to the bot, such as in the Koko matchmaking model. An SM user could be encouraged to initiate interaction with the user through targeted advertising or collaboration with the SM platform. This approach minimizes privacy risks to the user as well as optics risks to the builder, as engagement with the user is based on the user's consent. An interviewee representing an SM platform that used search redirects to invite at-risk users to reach out to human-manned resources reported that "thus far the feedback is exclusively positive" but stressed that sensitivities of the user base and responsibilities of the platform required careful balancing.[16] Another interviewee passed along the

Table 4.6
Variable Assessment: Activation

Option	Technical Feasibility	User Risk	Builder Risk
Deployer manually initiates			
User initiates			
Activity or user meets bot criteria			

NOTE: Activation models: bots activated by the deployer, bots that go active when a user requests, and smart bots that are activated by user/activity criteria. Green = proceed with confidence, yellow = proceed with caution, orange = proceed with extreme caution. Activation strategy, when analyzed in the absence of other factors, has no clear impact on program interoperability or potential impact.

[16] Interview with SM platform provider, November 18, 2016.

results of a survey in which recipients of a particular bot intervention from an SM platform said the intervention actually improved their affinity toward that platform—partially a testament to how carefully they crafted their invitations by matching language styles to their target audience and by testing their performance with analysis on user behavior.[17]

Alternatively, the trigger could be when SM activity meets certain criteria, such as a surge in posts with a particular hashtag, or when a user meets a set of criteria, such as when a user with a given percentage of tweets of interest reaches a certain follower count. This type of automated activation is more technically complicated to pull off successfully than user initiation and poses more privacy risks to the user and legal questions to the builder, taking human initiation out of the equation and opening the door to unintended interactions. On the other hand, automated rather than manual activation boosts the potential reach of a bot program in a scalable way.

How?

In this section, we examine the questions of how automated a bot program will be, how much it will rely on AI and DL, and how it will deal with data retention issues.

First, we ask the question, "To what extent is bot activity automated?" as summarized in Table 4.7.

The more a bot senses, decides, or acts without human oversight, the more automated a bot's activity becomes, and the more autonomy the bot can be said to have. This autonomy will tend to lower response times, increase scalability, and expand the scale of potential impact. However, particularly given technological limitations through 2017, increased automation may also decrease the quality of bot-target interactions, thereby limiting the depth of potential impact. Automation of bot activity will increase risk in crisis, imminent threat, or particularly delicate situations that may require human attention. Higher degrees of automation will increase indicators of bot-like activity and risk of detection, particularly during extended interactions. A director

---

[17] Interview with two bot industry experts, December 16, 2016.

Table 4.7
Variable Assessment: Automation

Option	Technical Feasibility	Builder Risk: Control	Potential Impact: Scalability	Potential Impact: Precision
Fully automated				
Human-in-the-loop				
Computer-in-the-loop				

NOTE: A range of bot automation from fully automated, some human involvement, and primarily human-driven with automated assist. Green = proceed with confidence, yellow = proceed with caution, orange = proceed with extreme caution. As with other variables, user risk varies too widely based on communication substance and tactics to meaningfully assess here, while interoperability between different involved actors remains relatively unaffected by automation decisions.

of an online CVE program argued that "intervention is a long process [involving] relationship building . . . getting to know the person [and] building trust" and ultimately determined: "In the intervention space, [the bots] would have to be teamed up with humans for effectiveness."[18]

In contrast with a fully automated bot, a human-in-the-loop model involves a bot closely overseen by humans, in which bots triage interactions and elevate more difficult decisions or critical situations to the level of human attention, balancing scalability with builder control and precision.[19] Further along the spectrum away from automation, a computer-in-the-loop model involves a human assisted by bots, such as when bots auto-suggest responses or actions for humans, increasing response times.

The second question we ask about how bots act is: wherever bot activity is automated and how much do bots rely on AI and DL, as opposed to rules-based algorithms like hard-coded decision trees? We summarize AI reliance options in Table 4.8.

---

[18] Interview with two online CVE intervention program directors, December 20, 2016.

[19] Interview with SM platform provider, November 18, 2016; interview with two bot industry experts, December 16, 2016.

Table 4.8
Variable Assessment: Reliance on Artificial Intelligence and Deep Learning

Dimension	Option	Technical Feasibility	Builder Risk: Control	Potential for Process Improvement
Reliance on AI	AI-based			
	Rules-based			
Reliance on AI by activity	Sense: AI			
	Decide: AI			
	Act: AI			

NOTE: Level of reliance on AI broadly or deep algorithmic machine learning. Green = proceed with confidence, yellow = proceed with caution, orange = proceed with extreme caution. Reliance on AI and DL has no clear impact on program interoperability between various stakeholders, while user risk is affected more by what is done to users than by the technical methods a bot uses to decide what to do to them.

Relying on programs based on AI and DL rather than rules-based algorithms embraces the potential of emerging technology to allow for process improvement and to act on insights not available to the human eye. In doing so, AI and DL may improve a bot's human disguise, the quality of a bot's one-on-one engagements, and the bot's ability to evade detection. However, reliance on AI and on-the-job ML also increases the risk of a bot going off script, engaging in legally, ethically, or materially problematic activity or in unforeseen behaviors that risk detection. As one interviewee put it, "A bot learning as it goes along. . . . [It] is subject to social influence [and] can be exploited by the other side. You need to make sure it's constrained. You don't want your counter-radicalization bots to become radicalized."[20]

Lastly, how much data is retained, and for how long? Various data retention options are summarized in Table 4.9.

As the amount and variety of data collected by a bot or botnet grows, so does the potential for a bot program to evade detection, bene-

[20] Interview with SM management tool provider, November 8, 2016.

Table 4.9
Variable Assessment: Data Retention

Option	Technical Feasibility	User Risk: Privacy	Builder Risk: Legal Liability	Potential Impact: Quality
Retain all permanently				
Retain all for a period				
Retain some permanently				
Retain some for a period				
Retain none				

NOTE: The length of time data from bot/user interactions is stored. Green = proceed with confidence, yellow = proceed with caution, orange = proceed with extreme caution. Data retention has no clear impact on complexity, in terms of how actors cooperate within a bot program.

fit from process improvement, and conduct intelligence collection. The convincingness of a bot's interactions relies in part on the bot's situational awareness and contextual memory. Building a bot that is able to successfully maintain a human disguise without retaining any data about the users it is interacting with would be an extremely technological challenge. Data retention also allows a bot program to use training logs for ML and, of course, is necessary for intelligence collection. However, more data retention also corresponds to increased requirements for technological storage and heightened liability for recording PII, other sensitive information, and attendant privacy violations.

At What Visibility?

Visibility considerations for bot programs include volume of operations, utilization of "human" disguises, and levels of attribution.

First, at what scale or volume of activity are bots operating? These scaling variables are summarized in Table 4.10.

Volume of activity is a key enabling factor for bots. The more bots are involved and the more often they act, the larger the potential magnitude of impact. Further, large numbers of bots working together, with a ready supply of reserve bots to replace accounts suspended for

Table 4.10
Variable Assessment: Volume

Option	Technical Feasibility	Builder Risk: Detection/ Attribution	Potential Impact: Breadth
High volume			
Medium volume			
Low volume			

NOTE: Both the total volume of bots and the volume of how active they are. Green = proceed with confidence, yellow = proceed with caution, orange = proceed with extreme caution. User risk varies too widely based on other factors to be meaningfully assessed here, while complexity in terms of program interoperability is not particularly affected by volume of communications.

bot-like behavior, is necessary for efforts like astroturfing or wide-scale efforts to push particular narratives.[21]

However, the larger the footprint of a bot network, the higher the risk of discovery, attribution, detection, and suspension from platforms. This is partially because a number of bot-detection algorithms rely on the perception of anomalies that rise above the usual signal-to-noise ratio. As one interviewee put it: "Volume is a significant criteria we're using to detect perceived bot activity. A lot of our algorithms . . . assume your whole goal is to achieve volume, more retweets, more impressions. If your goal is to be much more focused and deliberate and hide among noise, you'll be much, much harder to detect."[22] Another interviewee agreed, suggesting setting volume at the minimum effective level to achieve the objective: "A lot of the times, it's the scale that gets you caught."[23]

Second, to what extent are bots in a given program operating under a "human" disguise? Degree of humanness options are summarized in Table 4.11.

---

[21] Interview with bot industry expert with IC background, October 20, 2016.

[22] Interview with tech industry expert who liaises with USG clients and previously worked at DoD, December 15, 2016.

[23] Interview with government expert working on CVE and online radicalization, December 9, 2016.

Table 4.11
Variable Assessment: "Human" Disguise

Option	Builder Risk: Optics If Discovered	Builder Risk: Legal and ToS Liability	Potential Impact: Credibility	Technical Feasibility
Claim human				
Unstated				
Declare "botness"				

NOTE: The level of clarity that a bot is in fact a bot and not human. Green = proceed with confidence, yellow = proceed with caution, orange = proceed with extreme caution. "Human" disguises have no clear impact on interoperability. While it could be argued that disguising bot accounts as humans runs a greater risk to users in terms of eroding trust in fellow internet users, the risk to general SM users varies greatly depending on how the disguise is used, while risk to builders is dramatically affected in a more predictable manner despite variation in other program components.

If successfully maintained, a bot's "human" disguise increases its credibility with and ability to influence target audiences.[24] However, convincingly imitating human behavior across many sustained interactions over a longtime horizon is likely beyond the reach of technology as of 2017. Further, if a bot pretending to be a human is unmasked as a bot, the botched disguise destroys credibility with the target and elevates any blowback from attribution. As one interviewee warned: "Long term, if you use bots, it's going to get discovered."[25]

Additionally, the deception involved conflicts with the ToS agreements of most SM platforms, raising additional legal and ethical questions. Multiple interviewees stressed that transparency is key to credibility, suggesting that a legal and ethical basic standard for bots involves transparency about being bots.[26]

---

[24] Interview with academic expert with military cyber background, November 22, 2016.

[25] Interview with government expert working on CVE and online radicalization, December 9, 2016.

[26] Interview with tech industry expert, December 15, 2016; interview with government expert working on CVE and online radicalization, December 9, 2016.

Table 4.12
Variable Assessment: Attribution

Option	Builder Risk	Potential Impact: Credibility	Technical Feasibility
None			
Delayed: two-click			
Delayed: one-click			
Full			

NOTE: The clarity of attribution for the bot's deployer. Green = proceed with confidence, yellow = proceed with caution, orange = proceed with extreme caution. As with the "human" disguise variable, interoperability is not uniformly affected by attribution, and while some may argue that nonattribution exacerbates internet user trust issues, associated risks to general users vary widely based on how other variables are set.

Third, how directly is bot activity attributed to the government actor involved? We summarize these attribution options in Table 4.12.

Delayed attribution can occur at various stages. These can range from one-click attribution, such as when a Twitter profile's self-description states a USG affiliation, to two-click or beyond, such as when the Twitter profile bio states that the account in question belongs to a "CVE network" and directs the reader to a webpage, in which small print acknowledges USG involvement.

In general, attribution tends to lessen legal and ToS liabilities and lessen the severity of backlash from nonattributed accounts being discovered, which will always be a risk. However, attribution also makes a range of bot options impractical and unpalatable.

Attribution severely limits credibility among almost all potential target audiences, including Muslim anti-ISIL activists and individuals at risk of radicalization by ISIL.[27] As one interviewee put it, "Even if we had the perfect formula for what to say to [counter-radicalize] individuals, if it comes out that it's a USG botnet that's pushing this out, it

[27] Interview with academic expert with military cyber background, November 22, 2016; interview with bot industry expert with IC background, October 20, 2016.

loses all credibility."[28] A CVE program director asked, "If they're bots, why do they have to be affiliated? We all know trust would be lost for sure."[29] An expert on ISIL online activity simply said, "Anything that's attributed to the U.S. is pointless."[30]

Attribution also limits the range of actions open to a bot program, constraining a number of lines of efforts in terms of optics and entirely ruling out harvest or masquerade bot operations that rely on deceiving targets. As the ISIL expert quoted above pointed out, "The only way to establish authenticity in a community . . . is by adopting their language and point of view to a certain extent, which the U.S. can't do in an attributed way."[31]

In the next section, we ask the larger question of what tasks can be tackled by bot programs built from these various components and variables.

Categories of Social Bot Operations

We lay out 12 possible concepts of action for a bot program, most of which could be conducted simultaneously. While the above section on bot program variables homes in on specific ways a bot program could be constructed, this section considers the varying overarching aims that bot programs could have and strategies they could pursue. These concepts fall under three broad categories.

First, under the umbrella of social bot operations that intend to influence and inform a target audience, we explore concepts of action for matchmaker, influence, prompter, astroturf, and disinformation bots.

---

[28] Interview with government expert working on CVE and online radicalization, December 9, 2016.

[29] Interview with two online CVE intervention program directors, December 20, 2016.

[30] Interview with academic expert with history of advising USG on ISIL Twitter activity, November 7, 2016.

[31] Interview with academic expert with history of advising USG on ISIL Twitter activity, November 7, 2016.

Second, in the category of bots that attempt to degrade or disrupt VE networks, we present noise, policeman, exposer, zombie, and masquerade bots.

Third, in the category of bots meant to collect intelligence, we consider harvest and mousetrap bot operations.

Within each of these three categories we present a table that assesses each CONOP by four of the five top-level assessment criteria used above to analyze individual variables: technical feasibility, general user risks, builder risks, and potential impact. The fifth criterion used to analyze bot variables—complexity in terms of program interoperability—depends more on implementation specifics than overarching aims and strategy and so is not applied here.

Influence and Inform

The bot concepts in the influence and inform category of goals include matchmaker, influence, prompter, astroturf, and disinformation, which will all be explained and analyzed below. The options that appear most immediately feasible, in terms of both available technology and risk, are the matchmaker and prompter bot options, presented in Table 4.13.

Table 4.13
Concepts of Action: Influence and Inform

Option	Description	Technical Feasibility	General User Risks	Builder Risks	Potential Impact
Matchmaker	Connect support and at-risk communities				
Influence	Engage at-risk accounts one-on-one				
Prompter	Internal-facing bot auto-suggests responses				
Dis/inform	Broadcast beneficial messages				
Astroturf	Amplify exposure of anti-extremist content				

NOTE: Green = proceed with confidence, yellow = proceed with caution, orange = proceed with extreme caution.

Matchmaker

The task of a matchmaker bot program is to connect members of at-risk communities to human support. This approach is relatively technically feasible and less risky than many alternatives while still being potentially impactful.

In an example concept of operation, a self-identified bot offers resources and support to an at-risk population. The bot is attributable at the two-click level via an NGO. The bot may initiate interactions with users on platforms like Reddit or respond to user initiation as in the Koko peer emotional support model. In this model, user attention is caught and user initiation invited through targeted advertising or platform collaboration.

Another potential approach could match at-risk users with skilled human support, such as counselors or former foreign fighters, potentially enabling meaningful and highly effective interactions. A potential issue here is scalability; one interviewee representing an SM platform that directs at-risk users to resources reported: "When we do pilots with partners, we send a ton of traffic. We overwhelm their capabilities."[32] A more scalable model with less quality control could crowdsource support similarly to the Kokobot (as detailed in Chapter Three), combining anonymous support peer matchmaking with crowdsourced or bot-operated quality and controls.

The technical feasibility involved with this bot varies somewhat based on implementation. For instance, waiting for users to initiate interaction is much simpler, technologically speaking, than automatically detecting persons at risk for radicalization based on observable online behavior. However, the declared nature of the matchmaker bot avoids the technological challenge of maintaining a convincing human facade. One of the advantages of this concept is that, if scalable, it offers a way to connect at-risk individuals with humans who would presumably be more persuasive or helpful than a bot, alleviating the discovery risks and quality limitations that come with a human disguise. With the declared role of matchmaker between humans, a bot

---

[32] Interview with SM platform provider, November 18, 2016.

can self-identify as a bot without losing any credibility, limiting some optics concerns without necessarily sacrificing potential impact.

Prompter

The task of a prompter bot is to auto-suggest responses or posts for human operators of SM accounts. The scale of potential impact would be limited by the number of human operators involved, but this type of internally facing bot would be the least risky option of any explored in this chapter for both general users of SM and the builder of the program.

For instance, for a human user tasked with reaching out to individuals at risk for radicalization, an internal-facing bot could queue up three suggested Twitter replies for a given target, auto-filling the target's name and text tailored to interests the target has expressed via prior tweets. The human could choose one of the three options, modify it if desired, and click "send" or "post."

Also called a centaur approach, this human-machine pair enjoys several advantages over a human working alone. First, the auto-suggestions may increase human response time, efficiency, and even credibility and effectiveness. Because radicalized corners of the internet are often insular with their own idiosyncratic language patterns, terminology, and stylistic indicators, a bot trained on dialogue from a particular community may help operators communicate with more authentic voices, providing easy access for less-trained operators or perhaps incorporating machine insights not picked up on by even well-trained operators. And, data retention of the human's modification or selection of machine-generated responses can feed into ML models, as valuable training data for future auto-suggestions or autonomous bot activity further down the road.

At the same time, this bot program would minimize risk in terms of control, optics, and legal and ethical challenges. As all bot activity is inward facing, bots are prevented from engaging in problematic ways with the public. A prompter bot avoids the liability of a bot's "human" disguise, an autonomous bot's unattributed nature, and any optics risks associated with the bot's unmasking.

A prompter bot would not be risk free. Data retention may create some risk for the builder or deployer in terms of liability for PII collection. Any use of bots to boost nonattributed human-operated accounts would pose just as much risk as if nonattributed human-operated accounts ran on their own. If operated at conspicuously high volumes, these centaur accounts may still be accused of being bots, and the accusation may result in suspension or public backlash even if untrue. Still, in the context of the alternatives, the risks associated with this approach are the lowest of all those considered in this chapter.

Influence

The task of an influence bot program is to engage at-risk accounts one-on-one. The advisability of this approach varies widely according to implementation, which faces a fundamental trade-off between potential impact on the one hand and technical feasibility and risk on the other.

In an example approach, a bot scans SM and detects posts based on criteria such as interest in extremism as displayed through keywords, then sends counterextremist messages to those users. The program may have the bot engage in an ongoing conversation if those messaged users respond.

If operating under a human disguise to boost credibility and chance of persuasion, bots would need advanced language capabilities to avoid detection. Attributed accounts or "out" bots, which declare their "botness," are likely to have less credibility. However, bots that transparently provide factual information are less likely to raise legal and ethical questions than bots that seek to promote a narrative behind a false front.[33]

To minimize risk, a delayed-attribution "counterpoint bot" could announce itself as a bot intended to provide users with alternate information, minimizing backlash from detection.[34] Alternatively, to maximize the chance of potential impact through persuasion, a nonattrib-

---

[33] Interview with government expert working on CVE and online radicalization, December 9, 2016.

[34] Interview with tech industry expert, December 15, 2016.

uted bot could pretend to be an in-group human to influence a target, although the technical challenges of maintaining this deception may be considerable, and the disguise raises a number of legal and ethical concerns.

Dis/Inform

The task of a dis/information bot network is to broadcast beneficial messages. This type of program could run the risk of significant public backlash and would likely need to be strictly tailored to overseas audiences to avoid constituting domestic propagandizing.

For example, a network of nonattributed bots with "human" disguises could target extremist, opposition, or unrelated hashtags to dominate them with beneficial messages or share original content through curated follower networks. These beneficial messages could be specific narratives, such as news that the Iraqi government is returning displaced families to their homes in cities retaken from ISIL.

Impact would likely be constrained by a number of factors, such as the Twitter filter that keeps tweets from unverified accounts out of the "top" view of a hashtag. This filter means that people would have to look at hashtags in the "live" view in order to see the bots' content.

At the same time, the risk involved would be considerable. Human disguises generally violate platforms' ToS. Further, using nonattributed accounts to push messages may realize public fears of government propaganda and invite considerable public backlash if such a program is uncovered. This approach would require narrowly tailoring target audiences to minimize legal uncertainty. Risk could also be mitigated by presenting very factual information rather than skewed narratives or disinformation.[35]

Astroturf

The task of an astroturf bot network is to amplify exposure of preexisting anti-extremist content. While still presenting risks in terms of optics, legality, and ToS, this approach may come with less danger

[35] Interview with government expert working on CVE and online radicalization, December 9, 2016.

to the builder than disinformation while achieving a comparable or greater influence.

For instance, a network of bots can use nonattributed accounts and "human" disguises to create an impression of grassroots opposition to ISIL or support for causes antithetical to ISIL, such as tolerance. Accounts can target extremist or other hashtags to drown out extremist content with anti-ISIL content or hyperinflate the visibility of particular links or articles by retweeting, liking, and reposting content.

The theory of potential impact for astroturf bots would rely not on de-radicalizing anyone but rather on discouraging fence-sitters from radicalizing by creating or strengthening an impression of widespread opposition to extremism and drowning out adversary content. Any potential impact would be very limited if attempted by attributed bots that declare their "botness." The nonattributed, disguised nature of these accounts would create significant risks for the builder, raising legal, ethical, and ToS questions and potentially leading to hazardous optics.

Still, as opposed to original narratives pushed by disinformation, there may be more inherent credibility in the indigenous content amplified by astroturf bots and fewer parallels drawn to government propagandizing. Further, if these bots are built and operated with sufficient technical sophistication and without too large of a signature, they may be more likely to escape notice than masses of bots pushing their own messaging instead of subtly amplifying the conversation of others.

Degrade/Disrupt Violent Extremist Networks

Bots that can degrade or disrupt VE networks include noise, policeman, exposer, zombie, and masquerade bots. From this group, the exposer bot, intended to transparently "out" undercover bot or troll accounts, appears the most immediately practicable, combining technical feasibility with relatively low risk for both the builder and general populations of SM users. The policeman bot also has potential, the noise bot seems to have more risks than benefits, and the masquerade and zombie bots appear to be out of reach as of 2017. Table 4.14 summarizes these various concepts of action.

Table 4.14
Concepts of Action: Degrade/Disrupt Violent Extremist Networks

Option	Description	Technical Feasibility	General User Risks	Builder Risks	Potential Impact
Noise	Hijack extremist hashtags with unrelated spam				
Policeman	Detect and flag extremist accounts for takedown				
Exposer	"Out" other bot or troll accounts as bots or trolls				
Zombie	Take over opposing bot networks				
Masquerade	Serve as false targets for extremist recruiters				

NOTE: Green = proceed with confidence, yellow = proceed with caution, orange = proceed with extreme caution.

Noise

The noise bot attempts to drown out extremists on communication channels, for example, by using hashtags with opposing or neutral content. This approach appears to pose particularly high risk without offering correspondingly high rewards.

A group of noise bots could spam extremist hashtags to either drown out the information extremists are trying to disseminate or to get the hashtag removed from trending categories by triggering the platform's spam filters. Any implementer would need to expect high account turnover and cultivate large numbers of burner bots, as accounts engaging in high-volume spamming are more likely to be swiftly flagged for ToS violations.

Similar to disinformation bots, platform filters like Twitter's filter for unverified accounts in "top" view of hashtags may limit the degree to which extremist content is obscured by noise, as users would have to look in the "live" view to see the noise. Even if triggering a spam filter gets an extremist hashtag removed from the "Trends for you" trending bar, dedicated opponents can still access the hashtag channel or move to a new hashtag. These factors limit the utility of noise bots.

Further, this approach involves a considerable amount of risk. If accounts are attributed, high-profile bot spamming as a repeat and flagrant violation of ToS may increase tensions with SM platforms. If accounts are nonattributed, high-profile bot spamming may draw attention to the botnet and accelerate attempts to attribute the activity. As noise bots attempt to drown out communication so that people are unable to speak to each other, they would likely raise serious free speech concerns for organizations like the American Civil Liberties Union (ACLU), which already considers government activity on SM to have chilling effects on free speech.[36]

Exposer

An exposer bot "outs" other bot or troll accounts as managed accounts. This approach complements minimal risk with potentially meaningful impact in some contexts, such as efforts against Russian disinformation that is spread via sock puppet accounts.

In one possible concept of operation, models for detecting bot or troll networks could be seeded with human-selected training data of known bots or trolls until they can successfully identify usernames of sock puppet accounts. The exposer bots, which are attributed and open about their "botness," then reply to bot or troll posts or comments, "outing" the original posters as bots disguising themselves as humans or users writing under fake identities.

An exposer bot's potential impact would depend on its context. Some adversary communities, such as potential ISIL supporters, may not care if their information is being disseminated by a bot or troll. Other audiences, such as the targets of Russian disinformation, may. Russian trolls pretend to be U.S. citizens, leveraging the disguise for legitimacy among American target audiences. Human operators searching for and manually responding to counterfeit accounts would be hobbled by the vastness of adversary networks and limits on their response time; to effectively inoculate audiences against disinforma-

---

36 Linda Lye, "Twitter Subpoenas Chill Free Speech; Latest Example Is in San Francisco," *ACLU Free Future Blog*, January 2, 2013; Matt Cagle and Hugh Handeyside, "The Government Is Trying to Influence Speech on Social Media—But How?" *ACLU Free Future Blog*, May 26, 2016.

tion, the rebuttal discrediting the adversary account would have to be nearly immediate at a speed and scale that would demand automation. As a RAND examination of the psychology of Russian disinformation observed, "Information that is initially assumed valid but is later retracted or proven false can continue to shape people's memory and influence their reasoning."[37]

Technical feasibility would vary based on the balance of the detection arms race between automated detection of sock puppet accounts and sock puppet operators attempting to evade detection. However, a host of indicators can be used to create bot signatures and identify suspicious accounts.[38]

This approach would minimize a number of risks. The transparent model—based on attributed, botness-declared accounts and on exposing sock puppets' true nature—avoids many optics and platform ToS issues. Countering deceptive speech with more factual speech avoids many First Amendment concerns, empowering the general public in the effort to distinguish between disinformation and organic debate.

Policeman

The policeman bot detects and flags extremist accounts for takedown. This approach likely offers only marginal impact, as pro-ISIL users already have a difficult time evading suspension campaigns on public SM forums.

In one possible model, attributed bots that declare their "botness" could scan users' posts for keywords and signifiers of violence promotion and flag their accounts for suspension, reporting them for ToS violations.

This approach is within the realm of technical feasibility. Explicit calls for violence can generally be detected by machines, and developing computational approaches to detect extremist talk is relatively straightforward.[39] Pro-ISIL users already struggle to maintain accounts

---

[37] Christopher Paul and Miriam Matthews, *The Russian "Firehose of Falsehood" Propaganda Model: Why It Might Work and Options to Counter It*, Santa Monica, Calif.: RAND Corporation, PE-198-OSD, 2016, p. 6.

[38] Interview with SM management tool provider, November 8, 2016.

[39] Interview with SM management tool provider, November 8, 2016.

on Twitter against the pace of suspensions,[40] but the speed of automated flagging could further increase marginal costs. In addition, turning flagging into an automated process can allow human personnel to be repurposed to more fine-tuned operations.

However, there are risks associated with this approach, including infringements on First Amendment rights.[41] Some technology companies such as Twitter are beginning to quietly use automated detection measures,[42] but others lack the resources or worry about the associated optics and "slippery slope" of such monitoring and intervention.[43] Organizations such as the ACLU have argued that monitoring and automated takedowns have potentially chilling effects on free speech.[44]

Any government attempt to compel platforms to remove First Amendment–protected free speech, even if it violates the platforms' ToS, would almost certainly be considered an illegal end run around the U.S. Constitution. In seeking to remove content or block users, the USG is required to follow established legal procedures such as securing court orders.[45] While a private citizen can flag ToS violations for platform removal, government entities doing so might be perceived as engaging in coercion and censorship.[46]

Determining the fine line between legitimate expression of political views and incitement to violence can sometimes be difficult. Any approach that attempts to prevent a person from being able to speak in a public forum, rather than reporting specific ToS violations that person has committed, is more likely to run afoul of that line. As one interviewee asked, "Is it okay for [ISIL leader Abu Bakr] al-Baghdadi

---

[40] Interview with two online CVE intervention program directors, December 20, 2016.

[41] For example, *Zablocki v. Redhail* (1978); *Reno v. ACLU* (1997); interview with SM management tool provider, November 8, 2016; interview with two legal scholars focused on digital threats to civil society, December 19, 2016.

[42] Interview with two online CVE intervention program directors, December 20, 2016.

[43] Interview with SM platform provider, November 18, 2016.

[44] Lye, 2013; Cagle and Handeyside, 2016.

[45] *Zablocki v. Redhail* (1978); *Reno v. ACLU* (1997).

[46] Interview with two legal scholars focused on digital threats to civil society, December 19, 2016.

to talk about the weather?"[47] Further, a policy of pressuring SM platforms to remove objectionable content is, as one interviewee pointed out, "susceptible to abuse by governments that try to use their own determinations about what constitutes terrorism and terrorist-related content, to take down speech they disfavor."[48] This concern should be considered in the context of other international actors whose attempts to silence political opposition could be inadvertently normalized by USG behavior.

Zombie

The zombie approach involves taking over an opposing bot network. Both the risks and potential benefits of this type of bot operation largely depend on what is done with the bot network after it is taken over.

This type of bot program would need to first identify an adversary bot network then hack into the botnet, assert control over the bots, and redirect them. The "take-over" could likely last for only a limited amount of time, as the adversary would presumably either turn off or reassert control over its network. In the meantime, the program could control what the bots disseminate in order to distribute targeted disinformation or counterextremist messages. Alternatively, the program could burn the bot network by having the bots self-identify as bots or self-destruct their accounts.

The potential impact of burning the zombie network would be to limit its future utility to the adversary for recruitment or propaganda purposes. Repurposing the zombie network may have more direct impacts; counterextremist messages will hardly persuade individuals who are already listening to extremist bots, but targeted disinformation may have stronger or more insidious impacts on network degradation.[49]

The attendant risks for the program builder are extreme. If the zombie bot network is used to influence potential extremists, then seri-

---

[47] Interview with two online CVE intervention program directors, December 20, 2016.

[48] Interview with two legal scholars focused on digital threats to civil society, December 19, 2016.

[49] Interview with academic expert with military cyber background, November 22, 2016.

ous optics risks and legal issues will likely to come into play, in addition to any problematic international norms set by the hacking and sabotage.[50] However, if the zombie bot network is simply burned, the associated risks will be more limited.

Technical feasibility is highly dependent on the adversary's bot network but would in most cases probably strain the limits of technology through 2017. This is particularly true for any attempt to maintain or reanimate adversary bot networks in a manner that escapes notice by the adversary.

Masquerade

The task of masquerade bots is to serve as false targets for extremist recruiters. Considering this approach's lackluster potential impact, serious technological challenges, and weighty attendant risks, a masquerade bot program does not appear to be promising.

Masquerade bots could pose as targets for adversary influence, presumably by posting content that is friendly to the adversary's cause and either waiting for recruiters to make contact or reaching out directly to known extremist recruiters. This would require interagency clearance so as to avoid interfering with ongoing criminal or intelligence-collection operations. These same bots could be used to "harvest" intelligence, as discussed in the next section.

The potential impact would be to waste extremist recruiter time or begin to create distrust within the network, as recruiters may not know whether a potential recruit is a bot or a human. To justify the network creation efforts, there would have to be a lot of recruiters and many masquerade bots. This approach may not be technologically feasible; the capacity for multiple social bots to maintain human disguise through prolonged interaction at scale may be out of reach.

Further, a masquerade bot program would incur a number of risks. For instance, by posing as an ISIL supporter, a bot may actually promote ISIL causes. This would raise a number of legal and ethical questions, including entrapment and material support to terrorism,[51] not

---

[50] Interview with academic expert with military cyber background, November 22, 2016.

[51] Interview with two online CVE intervention program directors, December 20, 2016.

to mention fueling conspiracy theories if these bots were unmasked. However, a certain type of optics risk would likely be limited in this type of operation, as the target audience would be limited to ISIL recruiters. As one government official put it: "If you're just targeting ISIL recruiters, the general public probably won't mind."[52] Many of these risk considerations apply to both of the intelligence-gathering bot types discussed in the next section.

Collect Intelligence

The two types of intelligence-gathering bots discussed here are harvest bots, which attempt to friend targets to gather information available on their private profiles; and mousetrap bots, which attempt to leverage recruiter contact into invitations to closed VE networks. However, a single bot could operate as a masquerade bot, a harvest bot, or a mousetrap bot, based purely on how targets respond to the bot's engagement, as summarized in Table 4.15.

Harvest

As discussed above, a harvest bot's task is to engage with extremists to collect PII or any intelligence of interest that can be harvested from their private profiles.

Table 4.15
Concepts of Action: Collect Intelligence

Option	Description	Technical Feasibility	General User Risks	Builder Risks	Potential Impact
Harvest	Lure extremist engagement in order to collect PII				
Mousetrap	Serve as false recruitment targets to gain access to closed VE networks				

NOTE: Green = proceed with confidence, yellow = proceed with caution, orange = proceed with extreme caution.

[52] Interview with government expert working on CVE and online radicalization, December 9, 2016.

Similar to masquerade bots, nonattributed harvest bots could pose as extremist users or users at risk of radicalization by posting content friendly to the adversary's cause. These bots could wait for recruiters or other extremists to make contact or, more likely, attempt to friend or follow restricted extremist accounts. These bots could then be used to harvest intelligence, either passively by lurking to gather user profile information or actively by posting links to sites that will collect computer information.

Harvest bots could help map online networks of extremists for use in IO or gather their personal information for use in cyber or kinetic operations. As with masquerade bots, this type of operation would require interagency clearance to avoid interfering with ongoing criminal or intelligence-collection operations. Even with that precaution, however, the risks associated are extreme. The builder or deployer of the bot program risks ToS violations, legal challenges, and public backlash upon any attribution. Organizations such as the ACLU have already spoken out against USG intelligence-collection efforts on SM, citing chilling effects on free speech.[53] Even if the operation is narrowly targeted to adversary accounts, members of the general public may unwittingly fall prey to lures and traps, and the borderless nature of the internet makes restricting targeting only to non-U.S. residents technologically difficult.

Mousetrap

Mousetrap bots share much in common with harvest bots in that they pose as potential or actual extremists to collect intelligence but differ in that they aim to gain access to closed VE networks instead of general-use platforms and potentially act to sow disinformation rather than merely passively collecting information.

For instance, nonattributed bots could pose as ISIL supporters to score invitations to closed ISIL networks or channels. The bots could then lurk quietly in the background, collecting conversations from these private chatrooms. Once the bot's bona fides were established,

[53] Hugh Handeyside, "To the Government, Your Latest Facebook Rant Is Raw Intel," *ACLU Free Future Blog*, September 29, 2016; Lye, 2013.

the bot could attempt to change the tenor of conversations over time or to inject targeted disinformation.

At least as of 2017, social bot technology would not be able to support sustained interaction with skeptical extremists without raising suspicion of automation. However, this technological challenge could be sidestepped. One academic expert on ISIL SM activity suggested employing the human-in-the-loop model as soon as access to a closed network is gained: "As soon as that bot is confused for a real person and gets a DM [direct message] on Twitter or is invited to a private channel—that's when you'd alert the human officer, as it has become an intel asset."[54] He also suggested implementing this type of program within a "community large enough that people aren't evaluating individual users" and pointed out that when bots are cheap to create, scale can overwhelm low probabilities: "It's tactically similar to the Nigerian prince email scam—it doesn't need to work every time. The Nigerian prince email scam is usually deliberately not that sophisticated because you want to weed out people who are super skeptical."[55]

Potential impact would be variable. That this type of bot could detect operational attack planning seems unlikely though not impossible, as such planning would likely occur in more secure settings. However, this type of operation could also provide a valuable window into recruitment practices and targets and enable targeted disinformation to be introduced from within circles of trust.

All of the risks articulated above for masquerade and harvest bots—such as the difficulty of determining the U.S. person status of targets before collecting intelligence on them—apply to mousetrap bots as well. However, mousetrap bots would be particularly pressured to post problematic content, potentially raising issues of entrapment and material support to terrorism, in order to maintain their cover for an extended period of time.

---

[54] Interview with academic expert with history of advising USG on ISIL Twitter activity, November 7, 2016.

[55] Interview with academic expert with history of advising USG on ISIL Twitter activity, November 7, 2016.

An Example CONOP Assessment

Here we present an illustrative example of a full-fledged CONOP assessment. This example is a notional matchmaker bot program that seeks to provide resources for populations at risk for radicalization. This is a transparent matchmaker bot service, where users opt in through targeted advertising, and incorporates human-in-the-loop supervision. In our notional example, all relevant variables have been specified and assessed in Table 4.16.

This formulation for a matchmaker operation generally prioritizes transparency, minimizing risk for the builder and general SM user through user-initiated activation, no data retention, declared botness, and a target audience of non-U.S. adults. However, two-click attribution balances risk minimization with potential impact. All aspects are technologically feasible, although distinguishing non-U.S. persons from U.S. persons and engaging in multidirectional communication adds a challenge.

This is merely one example of how this variable and assessment framework can be used to think through many of the questions associated with designing a bot program. There is no simple answer to the question of which single bot program is most or least advisable; much depends on context: which options are chosen for each variable, who the extremist adversary is, how advanced a legal review has been done, and what priorities guide the builder or deployer.

However, a few relative observations can be made. Of bots that seek to influence and inform target audiences, the options that appear most feasible, in terms of both available technology and risk, are the matchmaker and prompter bot options. In terms of bots that attempt to degrade or disrupt VE networks, the exposer bot seems to be the most immediately practicable, combining technical feasibility with relatively low risk for both the builder and general populations of SM users. The policeman bot also has potential. For noise bots, risks seem to outweigh potential benefits, and masquerade and zombie bots appear to be out of reach for technology, at least as of 2017. As for bots that collect intelligence, harvest bots are the more technologically feasible option. However, no conceptual bot program is without risk, and no potential impact is guaranteed. Everything depends on implementation.

Table 4.16
Bot CONOP: Matchmaker

Question	Variable	Specification	Technical Feasibility	Builder Risk	User Risk	Potential Impact	Complexity
Who?	Deployer	NGO					
	Audience	Non-U.S. adults at risk for radicalization					
Where?	Platform	Public messenger platform					
What?	Communication breadth	Narrowcast					
	Communication depth	Interactive					
When?	Activation	User initiates, prompted by targeted advertising on Facebook					
How?	Automation	Human-in-the-loop					
	AI dependency	Rule-based					
	Data retention	None					
Visibility	Volume	N/A					
	Humanness	Declare botness					
	Attribution	Two-click					
Overall assessment							

CHAPTER FIVE

Recommendations

In this conclusion, we present recommendations on development and deployment of bot programs by USG actors and legal and ethical issues surrounding these bots. The following list summarizes our recommendations, which are then discussed in more detail in the rest of the chapter.

U.S. agencies should keep the following practical and technical considerations in mind and weigh the following contextual factors when contemplating and designing bot programs.

1. Leverage commercial development of bot technology, as industry investment in this rapidly evolving space has yielded significant progress.
2. Tailor bots to the environment in which they are to be deployed, such as platform structures of engagement or the culture of government censorship among the target audience; this will maximize credibility in sensitive contexts and help avoid disasters resulting from unanticipated mismatches.
3. Carefully craft the profile characteristics of proposed bots, as in-group avatars with high follower counts are more likely to attract positive engagement.
4. Pay attention to the network characteristics of users the bot is seeking to engage, such as the friend count of an individual target user or whether target users are connected merely by topic interest or preexist as a dense network of social connection; skeptical users are more likely to engage with accounts with whom they are already connected by social friends.

U.S. agencies should consider the following suggestions on how to mitigate the legal and ethical risks of any proposed bot program.

1. In light of the USG's leading role in the still rapidly evolving world of cyberspace, analyze the international precedent that may be set by any proposed bot program to avoid normalizing other states' invasive actions and behaviors that erode cybersecurity by interfering with the confidentiality, integrity, or availability of information online.
2. In response to concerns about the Establishment Cause, free speech, privacy, and the Smith-Mundt Act, focus engagement on narrowly targeted audiences of concern abroad, avoid targeting users based on religious criteria; and where deemed appropriate, erect firewalls between certain bot programs and law enforcement, intelligence agencies, or international partners.
3. With respect to the ToS issues of SM platforms, seek companies' permission before deploying bots whenever necessary and practicable.
4. Given the likelihood of U.S.-sponsored bot activities becoming public knowledge, make USG bot operations as transparent as possible, within operational constraints. This will help mitigate backlash and associated negative consequences.
5. To ensure legal compliance, we recommend specific legal review for each bot deployment operation under the applicable titles.

The USG should consider undertaking the following action items:

1. Communicate across agency lines about bot technology initiatives to develop a common conceptual framework and cross-agency operating picture.
2. Conduct a full interagency legal review regarding principles that USG bot programs should follow.
3. Promulgate doctrine about how USG actors intend to conduct operations to maximize transparency even while protecting sensitive operational details.

4. Test the efficacy and advisability of bot programs gradually by collaborating with NGOs or partner nations or by implementing an internal-facing bot program.
5. Promote bot-detection technologies to make it harder for adversaries to engage in bot-enabled deception.

Development and Deployment

Bots Are a Viable Approach

Our single most important conclusion from this report is that while bots are still an emerging technology, bot-based interventions are technically feasible and could plausibly have an impact on combating VE groups such as ISIL or disinformation and radicalization campaigns sponsored by foreign states. Bots are already being used successfully around the world in a number of relevant applications, are improving rapidly through research and development, and have enormous potential for many kinds of activities previously performed by humans.

The other side of this conclusion is that, while feasible, bot interventions are fraught with potential difficulty and risks. Microsoft's Tay is an object lesson in the kind of perverse outcomes an autonomous bot can yield, and as our SME interviews show, there is significant risk in how USG-sponsored bot interventions could be perceived. For these reasons, we recommend that where the potential return in reducing extremism is relatively high and the risks relatively low, the USG invest in developing and deploying bot technology in legally and ethically responsible ways.

Account for Risk to Reward

Another key conclusion of our report is that bots are a potentially transformational technology. Bots show promise for automating some kinds of human information-sharing and interaction tasks and leveraging human capability in high-context areas unsuited for automation. Accordingly, the potential reward is high. But risks are high as well in terms of how bot programs are perceived publicly, how they normalize international cyber conduct, how they may result in perverse or unintended outcomes, and so on. In Chapter Four of this report, we offered criteria for risk, feasibility, and impact assessment. We suggest making such assessments a regular part of any bot development and deployment planning process.

Account for Context

Our case studies highlight the importance of contextual factors for bot program design. These include the profile characteristics of a social bot such as apparent social influence and group identity; the level of bot activity and method of generating posts; the network characteristics of users that a bot is attempting to befriend or influence; and the platforms, cultures, and governmental regimes in which a bot is deployed.

This last set of contextual factors matters greatly, as shown by the case study of Microsoft chatbots Tay and Xiaoice. Xiaoice was successfully deployed on a private Chinese messenger app within a particular cultural and material context amenable to expected (and pro-social) interactions with the wider digital audience. Essentially the same technology was deployed in a U.S. context on a public forum, resulting in unexpected and extremely antisocial interactions. Contextual issues with platforms go beyond formal service terms and into the territory of platform culture; different platforms have user communities with different embedded assumptions. For example, Facebook is essentially attributable: users have to verify their identity, can have only one account, are required to use their real name, and must have a profile picture. This contrasts strongly with a platform like Tumblr, which has built-in assumptions about anonymity.

What works well in one context may go disastrously awry in another context, and there is a danger in concentrating on specific technology performance without accounting for context. Given this, we recommend any programs meant to develop and deploy bots explicitly include context evaluations as part of any risk to reward analysis.

Develop a Common Operating Picture and Vocabulary

One of the main outputs from this report is a set of concepts and terms for thinking and talking about bot types and bot-based interventions.

These include conceptual frameworks for bot technology and capabilities, operating concepts for employment, and terms for technology and functions. We think a common operating picture and vocabulary will help the USG as it crafts and deploys bots, particularly in terms of communication and coordination across the interagency. The proposed vocabulary and conceptual frameworks in this report are not meant to be final or definitive, and it is likely that new developments in technology or within the wider security context will necessitate updates and additions to the terms and concepts here. But a common way of thinking and talking about bots will be an important enabler in the development and successful deployment of counterextremist bot programs. We recommend the sponsors of the project advocate for this common operating picture by distributing this report to policymakers, supported users, and vendors and by engaging in a cross-agency conversation about the questions it raises, ideally facilitating coordination of bot development efforts across any USG agencies that might otherwise be unaware of the other's potential engagement with the topic.

Leverage Commercial Development

The enormous promise of bot technology means that industry is pouring resources into research and development for bots. A useful framework promulgated at the Microsoft-funded O'Reilly Bot Day conference, attended by research staff, was that bots are the fourth digital wave: a revolution in desktop computers, followed by the internet revolution, followed by the explosion of mobile technology and platforms, now giving way to a wave in bot technology. In the three previous technology waves, the USG generally leveraged industry innovation rather than directly funding research and development (the Advanced Research Projects Agency Network notwithstanding). We think that the USG can pursue a similar course here and should look for ways to agilely and effectively adapt commercial bot systems when possible.

Favor Detection over Disguise

Many of the SMEs we interviewed described an ongoing competition between bot-detection methods and technology on the one hand and bot disguise methods and technology on the other. Interviewees described this contest as an "arms race" that detection was currently winning, but it is likely to shift back and forth over time. We think that the question of which side of this arms race is winning has stakes for the USG. A more transparent world, in which extremists or nation-state adversaries have difficulty using bots in deceptive ways, such as synthesizing false video of U.S. leaders, is likely a safer world. So while we acknowledge that the United States might legitimately have specific needs for disguised bot operations, in general it is better off funding and developing bot-detection technologies.

Legal and Ethical Issues

In light of the many complex legal and ethical issues raised by any U.S. application of bot technology, the USG should conduct a full interagency legal review regarding principles that USG bot programs should follow. USG actors should also consider developing and publicly promulgating doctrine about how they intend to conduct bot operations to maximize transparency even while protecting sensitive operational details.

International Precedent Setting

The United States has a leadership role in the international community, so actions the United States takes in novel spaces such as bot deployment may set enduring precedents. Bots that interfere with the confidentiality, integrity, or availability of information might be seen as undermining cybersecurity. In such a case, the United States runs the risk of setting precedents that normalize other states' pernicious actions. Given this, RAND recommends risk analyses for bot deployment that include how any operation or program sets international precedent in cyberspace.

First Amendment Considerations

The USG is prohibited by the Establishment Clause from taking actions that favor one religion over another. Bot programs raise the risk that well-intentioned efforts to engage non-U.S. audiences could unintentionally target U.S. citizens on the basis of their religion. As an example, we can imagine a bot program that looks for online discussion forums for a religious group vulnerable to radicalization and that offers alternative resources from moderate sects of that group. This kind of engagement with U.S. citizens could be construed as the promotion of a particular version of a religion. Alternatively, targeting users for negative attention on the basis of religious affiliation raises similar questions of religious freedom. To mitigate these risks, U.S. agencies designing bot programs should attempt to use behavioral, political, and cultural-based criteria when deciding whether to engage with users rather than religion-based targeting criteria.

Other constitutional concerns raised by potential bot programs include infringement on privacy of U.S. persons and protected categories of free speech, not to mention the restrictions on any USG messaging intended for domestic audiences that are laid out in the Smith-Mundt Act. As a result of all these considerations, including the Establishment Clause, any U.S. agency contemplating a bot program should consider restricting target audiences to narrowly defined communities abroad. This might involve using geo-tagging and geo-inferencing methods and specifying particular language discriminants, as well as other indicators of location or U.S. personhood.

Potential USG deployers of bot programs such as the U.S. State Department should consider implementing firewalls with law enforcement or intelligence agencies, particularly for those programs focused on counter-radicalization rather than CT. As an ethical question, even designers of bot programs explicitly for intelligence-gathering purposes may wish to consider protecting information gathered by bots from international partners with different levels of human rights and privacy protections.

Platform Terms of Service

Bots are deployed on SM platforms such as Twitter and Facebook, and those platforms have a range of service terms that users agree to when they use the platform. The USG must take into account companies' ToS, as many limit bot activity. This raises a difficult proposition, in that there may be unavoidable tensions between operational efficacy and a desire to respect platforms' ToS. We can imagine many potentially valuable and (in and of themselves) ethical bot operations that would be prohibited by ToS restrictions. To mitigate this, we recommend, when necessary and possible, seeking companies' permission before bot deployment.

Transparency

Many of the experts we interviewed stressed both the potential negative consequences of USG-sponsored bot activities becoming public knowledge and the inevitability of that happening. We heard multiple variations of "It's a matter of when, not if"—that is, when USG sponsorship of a bot program becomes public. SMEs also repeatedly pointed out that many potentially valuable bot programs would automatically be rejected or rendered ineffective if they were understood to be USG-sponsored programs. This again raises the issue of tensions between operational efficacy and public reception, including long-term damage to U.S. credibility. Potential ways to mitigate this risk include the USG making bot activities as transparent as possible. If a bot program can still function with transparency, that should be the default approach.

Indirect or Partial Alternatives

One strategy for mitigating legal and ethical risk involves testing out bot programs internally or via partners rather than diving into full-blown USG deployment of autonomous bot programs.

The USG may wish to support NGOs or partner nations engaged in anti-extremist activities with bot technology, so as to create a remove between themselves and potentially impactful efforts.[1] This may have an added practical benefit of boosting effectiveness, as USG credibility with desired target audiences is often extremely low. A matchmaker bot connecting at-risk individuals to support communities is a prime candidate for collaboration with NGOs, as the effectiveness of the matchmaker CVE concept would be best served, in terms of effective-

[1] We note that our report did not include a legal review, and the question of how much support the USG can give to partners, without in effect contracting out its actions, is not clear.

ness and user risk, by a deployer that can credibly claim to be insulated from U.S. law enforcement and intelligence agencies.

Lastly, the USG should consider inward-facing bot programs, such as a prompter bot. As described in Chapter Four, this type of bot would auto-suggest posts or replies for human operators of SM accounts. Such in-house programs have much lower risks of negative public reception but could still constitute extremely valuable efficiency-boosting interventions. They would also serve as valuable sources of training data for future, more autonomous bot programs.

Legal Review for Specific Bot Operations

Our report revealed a potential tension between the operational needs of CVE practitioners and legal considerations in USG messaging. Overt attribution of messaging to the USG is a way to exercise restraint and err on the side of caution in engaging in IO, but such attribution can undermine the effectiveness of messaging. While our report clearly notes there are serious legal considerations for the USG in conducting CVE messaging with regard to bot deployment, we also note that USG is legally permitted to take action against foreign IO operations—for example, in U.S. military action in support of established Title 10 missions or the GEC's broad mandate to lead and coordinate USG efforts to counter the influence of VE and terrorist organizations. Given this, we recommend specific legal review for each bot deployment operation under the applicable titles.

Conclusions

Our report finds that the state of bot development through 2017 presents a viable approach for a range of technologically feasible, plausibly impactful interventions. However, decisionmakers must carefully weigh the expected rewards of any proposed bot program against the many risks associated with automated interventions. The USG should also consider promoting bot-detection technology to make it harder for adversaries to engage in bot-enabled deception. Other insights include the importance and potential value of accounting for contextual factors in bot program design, developing a common conceptual framework and cross-agency operating picture, and leveraging commercial development in this area.

Our report also suggests a range of strategies for mitigating the considerable risks posed by USG-deployed bots. Given the wide range of complex legal and ethical issues raised by bots, we first suggest that the USG conduct a full legal interagency review. In light of the USG's leading role in the still rapidly evolving world of cyberspace, we recommend analyzing the international precedent set by any proposed bot program. In response to concerns about the Establishment Cause, free speech, privacy, and the Smith-Mundt Act, we recommend focusing engagement on narrowly targeted audiences abroad; avoiding targeting users based on religious criteria; and where deemed appropriate, erecting firewalls between certain bot programs and law enforcement, intelligence agencies, or international partners. With respect to SM platform's ToS issues, we recommend seeking companies' permission before deploying bots whenever necessary and possible. In the context of the seeming inevitability and negative consequences of U.S.-sponsored bot activities becoming public knowledge, we recommend making USG bot operations as transparent as possible. Lastly, to test the efficacy or advisability of bot programs, we recommend potentially collaborating with NGOs or partner nations or implementing internal bot programs.

APPENDIX A

Technology Review: Methods and Goals

To develop a basis of knowledge regarding social bots, our literature review of research (as of 2017) had two components. The review's first goal was to learn about the different types of social bots and how they are used. To conduct this section of the review, Google Scholar was used as a starting point for information-gathering. The word "bot" was used as a starting term, with words such as "social," "Twitter," "Facebook," "network," "chat," "ethics," and "influence" added on to refine results. Using this method, a number of references were discovered that fit the profile of this project. By examining the bibliographies of these sources, it became clear that many of the works seemed to reference a core set of sources, including those by Ratkiewicz and Boshmaf. The references from these authors were then scanned for additional sources on bots and for sources on the influence of SM and social networks more broadly. The types of bots that came up frequently in this research and in subject-matter interviews were then broken down into a number of categories. With these categories in mind, news and magazine articles that referenced specific bot types were used to find specific cases where these types of bots have been employed. Finally, cases that did not involve bots but where social networks were used to cause an impact were examined to broaden the search. When cases that seemed applicable and could potentially be achieved through the use of bots were found, they were added to the literature review.

The second goal of the review was to examine how bots are built. This information was gleaned from a survey of papers posted on Cornell University's arxiv.org (a preprint repository favored by computer science and AI practitioners), the API documentation offered by SM platforms such as Twitter and Facebook, and software repositories including GitHub and the Python Package Index. Arxiv.org was searched for terms relating to bots and SM as it contains the most up-to-date papers available to the public. While arxiv.org did not have a large number of preprint papers on these topics, many cited below have been published, and final versions are cited wherever possible. When examining the API documentation for SM platforms, a particular interest was ascertaining these firms' policies on using their APIs for bots and the difficulty of doing so. Links to the API libraries are often available in the developer documentation provided by SM platforms, while others were found by searching software repositories.

References

Abokhodair, Norah, Daisy Yoo, and David McDonald, "Dissecting a Social Botnet: Growth, Content and Influence in Twitter," *Proceedings of the 18th ACM Conference on Computer Supported Cooperative Work & Social Computing*, New York: Association for Computing Machinery, March 2015. As of May 16, 2017: http://dl.acm.org/citation.cfm?id=2675208

Aiello, Luca Maria, Matrina Deplano, Rossano Schifanella, and Giancarlo Ruffo, "People Are Strange When You're a Stranger: Impact and Influence of Bots on Social Networks," *Proceedings of the Sixth International AAAI Conference on Weblogs and Social Media*, Menlo Park, Calif.: Association for the Advancement of Artificial Intelligence, 2012. As of May 22, 2017: https://www.aaai.org/ocs/index.php/ICWSM/ICWSM12/paper/viewFile/4523/4961

Aro, Jessikka, "The Cyberspace War: Propaganda and Trolling as Warfare Tools," *European View*, Vol. 15, No. 1, June 2016, pp. 121–132. As of May 22, 2017: https://link.springer.com/article/10.1007/s12290-016-0395-5

Boshmaf, Yazan, Ildar Muslukhov, Konstantin Beznosov, and Matei Ripeanu, "The Socialbot Network: When Bots Socialize for Fame and Money," *Proceedings of the Twenty-Seventh Annual Computer Security Applications Conference*, New York: Association for Computing Machinery, 2011. As of April 7, 2017: http://lersse-dl.ece.ubc.ca/record/264/files/264.pdf

———, "Design and Analysis of a Social Botnet," *Computer Networks: The International Journal of Computer and Telecommunications Networking*, Vol. 2, No. 57, February 2013, pp. 556–578. As of May 22, 2017: http://dl.acm.org/citation.cfm?id=2450801

Brandenburg v. Ohio, 315 U.S. 568 (1969). As of May 23, 2017: https://www.law.cornell.edu/supremecourt/text/395/444

Brown, Jesse, "Attack of the Bimbots," *McLeans*, June 10, 2011. As of May 22, 2017: http://www.macleans.ca/society/technology/attack-of-the-bimbots/

Bruner, Jon, "Lili Cheng on Bot Personalities," *O'Reilly*, September 29, 2016. As of April 7, 2017:
https://www.oreilly.com/ideas/lili-cheng-on-bot-personalities

Butt, Craig, and Thomas Hounslow, "Spambots Target Tweeting Pollies," *Sydney Morning Herald*, April 28, 2013. As of September 14, 2019:
https://www.smh.com.au/technology/spambots-target-tweeting-pollies-20130429-2inim.html

BuyAccs.com, "Buy Bulk Accounts at Best Prices," website, undated. As of September 15, 2019:
https://buyaccs.com

Cagle, Matt, and Hugh Handeyside, "The Government Is Trying to Influence Speech on Social Media—But How?" *ACLU Free Future Blog*, May 26, 2016. As of April 17, 2017:
https://www.aclu.org/blog/free-future/government-trying-influence-speech-social-media-how

Chaplinsky v. New Hampshire, 315 U.S. 568 (1942). As of May 23, 2017:
https://www.law.cornell.edu/supremecourt/text/315/568

Chapman, Matthew, "A Health App's AI Took on Human Doctors to Triage Patients," *Vice*, June 7, 2016. As of September 14, 2019:
https://www.vice.com/en_us/article/z43354/a-health-apps-ai-took-on-human-doctors-to-triage-patients

Charlton, Alistair, "Microsoft Tay AI Returns to Boast of Smoking Weed in Front of Police and Spam 200k Followers," *International Business Times*, March 30, 2016. As of May 23, 2017:
http://www.ibtimes.co.uk/microsoft-tay-ai-returns-boast-smoking-weed-front-police-spam-200k-followers-1552164

Chen, Adrian, "The Agency," *New York Times Magazine*, June 2, 2015. As of May 23, 2017:
http://www.nytimes.com/2015/06/07/magazine/the-agency.html

Cheng, Lili, "Bots in Society," *O'Reilly Bot Day Conference Proceedings*, October 19, 2016. As of May 23, 2017:
https://conferences.oreilly.com/artificial-intelligence/bot-ca/public/schedule/proceedings

Cho, Kyunghyun, "Natural Language Understanding with Distributed Representation," lecture note for DS-GA 3001, "Natural Language Understanding with Distributed Representation," delivered at Center for Data Science, New York University, November 24, 2015. As of May 22, 2017:
https://arxiv.org/abs/1511.07916

Coldewey, Devin, "Researchers Flood Facebook with Bots, Collect 250GB of User Data," *Tech Crunch*, November 1, 2011. As of May 22, 2017:
https://techcrunch.com/2011/11/01/researchers-flood-facebook-with-bots-collect-250gb-of-user-data/

Cook, David, Benjamin Waugh, Maldini Abdipanah, Omid Hashemi, and Shaquille Abdul Rahman, "Twitter Deception and Influence: Issues of Identity, Slacktivism, and Puppetry," *Journal of Information Warfare*, Vol. 13, No. 1, 2014. As of May 22, 2017:
https://works.bepress.com/david_cook/15/

Cornell University, "Establishment Clause," webpage, Legal Information Institute, Cornell University Law School, undated. As of May 23, 2017:
https://www.law.cornell.edu/wex/establishment_clause

Dafoe, Allan, and Stuart Russell, "Yes, We Are Worried About the Existential Risk of Artificial Intelligence," *MIT Technology Review*, November 2, 2016. As of May 22, 2017:
https://www.technologyreview.com/s/602776/yes-we-are-worried-about-the-existential-risk-of-artificial-intelligence/

Davis, Clayton, Onur Varol, Emilio Ferrara, Alessandro Flammini, and Filippo Menczer, "BotOrNot: A System to Evaluate Social Bots," *Proceedings of the 25th International Conference Companion on World Wide Web*, New York: Association for Computing Machinery, February 2, 2016. As of May 22, 2017:
https://arxiv.org/pdf/1602.00975.pdf

Dewey, Caitlin, "I Created the Caitlyn Jenner bot @she_not_he. This Is What I Learned," *Washington Post*, June 2, 2015. As of May 22, 2017:
https://www.washingtonpost.com/news/the-intersect/wp/2015/06/02/i-created-the-caitlyn-jenner-bot-she_not_he-this-is-what-i-learned/

———, "This Bot Expertly Baits Internet Imbeciles into Losing Arguments," *Washington Post*, October 5, 2016. As of May 22, 2017:
https://www.washingtonpost.com/news/the-intersect/wp/2016/10/05/this-bot-expertly-baits-internet-imbeciles-into-losing-arguments/

Duggan, Maeve, Nicole Ellison, Cliff Lampe, Amanda Lenhart, and Mary Madden, "Social Media Update 2014," *Pew Research Center*, January 9, 2015. As of May 22, 2017:
http://www.pewinternet.org/2015/01/09/social-media-update-2014/

Edwards, Chad, Autumn Edwards, Patric Spence, and Ashleigh Shelton, "Is That a Robot Running the Social Media Feed? Testing the Differences in Perceptions of Communication Quality for a Human Agent and a Bot Agent on Twitter," *Computers in Human Behavior*, Vol. 33, April 2014, pp. 372–376. As of May 15, 2017:
https://doi.org/10.1016/j.chb.2013.08.013

Elyashar, Aviad, Michael Fire, Dima Kagan, and Yuval Elovici, "Homing Socialbots: Intrusion on a Specific Organization's Employee Using Socialbots," *Proceedings of the 2013 IEEE/ACM International Conference on Advances in Social Networks Analysis and Mining*, New York: Association for Computing Machinery, August 2013. As of May 22, 2017:
http://ieeexplore.ieee.org/stamp/stamp.jsp?arnumber=6785878

Etzioni, Oren, "No, the Experts Don't Think Superintelligent AI Is a Threat to Humanity," *MIT Technology Review*, September 20, 2016. As of May 22, 2017:
https://www.technologyreview.com/s/602410/no-the-experts-dont-think-superintelligent-ai-is-a-threat-to-humanity/

Europol, "Europol Internet Referral Unit One Year On," press release, The Hague, The Netherlands, July 22, 2016. As of May 23, 2017:
https://www.europol.europa.eu/newsroom/news/europol-internet-referral-unit-one-year

Facebook, "Documentation," Facebook for Developers, undated. As of November 21, 2016:
https://developers.facebook.com/docs/

———, "Facebook Platform Policy," Facebook for Developers, undated. As of May 23, 2017:
https://developers.facebook.com/policy/

Feifer, Jason, "Who's That Woman in the Twitter Bot Profile?" *Fast Company*, August 8, 2012. As of May 22, 2017:
https://www.fastcompany.com/3000064/whos-woman-twitter-bot-profile

Ferrara, Emilio, Onur Varol, Clayton Davis, Filippo Menczer, and Alessandro Flammini, "The Rise of Social Bots," *Communications of the ACM*, Vol. 59, No. 7, 2016, pp. 96–104. As of May 22, 2017:
https://arxiv.org/abs/1407.5225

Finley, Klint, "Pro-Government Twitter Bots Try to Hush Mexican Activist," *Wired*, August 23, 2015. As of May 23, 2017:
https://www.wired.com/2015/08/pro-government-twitter-bots-try-hush-mexican-activists/#slide-1

Forelle, Michelle, Phil Howard, Adres Monroy-Hernandez, and Saiph Savage, *Political Bots and the Manipulation of Public Opinion in Venezuela*, July 25, 2015. As of May 22, 2017:
https://ssrn.com/abstract=2635800

Freedom House, *Freedom of the Net 2016—Silencing the Messenger: Communication Apps Under Pressure*, Washington, D.C.: Freedom House, November 2016. As of May 23, 2017:
https://freedomhouse.org/report/freedom-net/freedom-net-2016

Freitas, Carlos, Fabricio Benevenuto, Saptarshi Ghosh, and Adriano Veloso, "Reverse Engineering Socialbot Infiltration Strategies in Twitter," Cornell University arXiv:1405.4927 [cs.SI], May 20, 2014. As of May 18, 2017:
https://arxiv.org/abs/1405.4927

Furnas, Alexander, and Devin Gaffney, "Statistical Probability That Mitt Romney's New Twitter Followers Are Just Normal Users: 0%," *Atlantic*, July 31, 2012. As of May 16, 2017:
https://www.theatlantic.com/technology/archive/2012/07/statistical-probability-that-mitt-romneys-new-twitter-followers-are-just-normal-users-0/260539/

Gallagher, Erin, "Bots Are Waging a Dirty War in Mexican Social Media," video, Media.ccc.de, August 15, 2015. As of May 23, 2017:
https://media.ccc.de/v/camp2015-6795-mexican_botnet_dirty_wars

Ghallab, Malik, Dana Nau, and Paolo Traverso, *Automated Planning and Acting*, New York: Cambridge University Press, 2016. As of May 22, 2017:
http://projects.laas.fr/planning/

Giles, Keir, *Russia's "New" Tools for Confronting the West: Continuity and Innovation in Moscow's Exercise of Power*, London, U.K.: Chatham House, Russia and Eurasia Programme, March 2016. As of April 5, 2017:
https://www.chathamhouse.org/sites/files/chathamhouse/publications/2016-03-russia-new-tools-giles.pdf

Gompf, Andrea, "Was the #Yamecansé Hashtag Hijacked by EPN Twitter Bots?" *Remezcla*, 2014. As of May 23, 2017:
http://remezcla.com/culture/was-yamecanse-hashtag-hijacked-by-epn-bots/

Grant, Katie, "Random Darknet Shopper: Exhibition Featuring Automated Dark Web Purchases Opens in London," *The Independent*, December 12, 2015. As of August 23, 2017:
http://www.independent.co.uk/life-style/gadgets-and-tech/news/random-darknet-shopper-exhibition-featuring-automated-dark-web-purchases-opens-in-london-a6770316.html

Gregory, Paul Roderick, "Inside Putin's Campaign of Social Media Trolling and Faked Ukrainian Crimes," *Forbes*, May 11, 2014. As of May 22, 2017:
https://www.forbes.com/sites/paulroderickgregory/2014/05/11/inside-putins-campaign-of-social-media-trolling-and-faked-ukrainian-crimes/

Gross, Doug, "On Twitter, a Curious Spike for Romney," CNN, July 24, 2012. As of May 23, 2017:
http://www.cnn.com/2012/07/24/tech/social-media/mitt-romney-twitter-followers/index.html

G20, "G20 Leaders' Communiqué," Antalya Summit, Turkey, November 16, 2015. As of May 23, 2017:
http://g20.org.tr/g20-leaders-commenced-the-antalya-summit/

Handeyside, Hugh, "To the Government, Your Latest Facebook Rant Is Raw Intel," *ACLU Free Future Blog*, September 29, 2016. As of April 17, 2017:
https://www.aclu.org/blog/free-future/government-your-latest-facebook-rant-raw-intel

Haughom, Jaclyn, "Combatting Terrorism in a Digital Age: First Amendment Implications," *Freedom Forum Institute*, November 16, 2016. As of September 14, 2019:
https://www.freedomforuminstitute.org/first-amendment-center/topics/freedom-of-speech-2/internet-first-amendment/combatting-terrorism-in-a-digital-age-first-amendment-implications/

Holder v. Humanitarian Law Project, 561 U.S. 1 (2010). As of May 23, 2017: https://www.supremecourt.gov/opinions/09pdf/08-1498.pdf

Horton, Helena, "Microsoft Deletes 'Teen Girl' AI After It Became a Hitler-Loving Sex Robot Within 24 Hours," *Telegraph*, March 24, 2016. As of April 7, 2017:
http://www.telegraph.co.uk/technology/2016/03/24/microsofts-teen-girl-ai-turns-into-a-hitler-loving-sex-robot-wit/

Howard, Philip, and Bence Kollanyi, "Bots, #StrongerIn, and #Brexit: Computational Propaganda During the UK-EU Referendum," Cornell University arXiv:1606.06356 [cs.SI], June 20, 2016. As of May 22, 2017: https://arxiv.org/abs/1606.06356

Jacobson v. United States, 503 U.S. 540 (1992). As of May 23, 2017: https://www.oyez.org/cases/1991/90-1124

Kik, "Terms of Service," webpage, February 1, 2017. As of May 23, 2017: https://www.kik.com/terms-of-service/

Kollanyi, Bence, Philip Howard, and Samuel Woolley, "Bots and Automation over Twitter During the First U.S. Presidential Debate," Data Memo 2016.2, Oxford, UK: Project on Computational Propaganda. As of May 22, 2017: http://philhoward.org/bots-and-automation-over-twitter-during-the-second-u-s-presidential-debate/

Lally, Adam, and Paul Fodor, "Natural Language Processing with Prolog in the IBM Watson System," *Association for Logic Program*, March 31, 2011. As of May 22, 2017:
https://www.cs.nmsu.edu/ALP/2011/03/natural-language-processing-with-prolog-in-the-ibm-watson-system/

Lye, Linda, "Twitter Subpoenas Chill Free Speech; Latest Example Is in San Francisco," *ACLU Free Future Blog*, January 2, 2013. As of April 17, 2017: https://www.aclu.org/blog/twitter-subpoenas-chill-free-speech-latest-example-san-francisco

Mack, Heather, "Cognitive Therapy Startup Koko Raises $2.5m, Launches Chatbot with Kik Messaging Service," *Mobi Health News*, August 9, 2016. As of May 22, 2017:
http://www.mobihealthnews.com/content/cognitive-therapy-startup-koko-raises-25m-launches-chatbot-kik-messaging-service

Marechal, Nathalie, "When Bots Tweet: Toward a Normative Framework for Bots on Social Networking Sites," *International Journal of Communication*, Vol. 10, 2016. As of May 23, 2017:
http://ijoc.org/index.php/ijoc/article/view/6180

Markoff, John, and Paul Mozur, "For Sympathetic Ear, More Chinese Turn to Smartphone Program," *New York Times*, August 4, 2015. As of April 5, 2017: https://www.nytimes.com/2015/08/04/science/for-sympathetic-ear-more-chinese-turn-to-smartphone-program.html

Marshall, Matt, "Sensay, a Chatbot for Getting Help with Any Task, Passes 1 Million Users," *Venture Beat*, May 5, 2016. As of May 22, 2017:
http://venturebeat.com/2016/05/05/
sensay-a-chatbot-for-getting-help-with-any-task-passes-1-million-users/

Metaxas, Panagiotis, and Eni Mustafaraj, "Social Media and the Elections," *Science*, Vol. 338, October 26, 2012, pp. 472–473. As of May 16, 2017:
http://science.sciencemag.org/content/sci/338/6106/472.full.pdf?sid=57f6d8b2
-35f6-4c57-bbaf-fd16067c2896

Metropolitan Police, "250,000th Piece of Online Extremist/Terrorist Material to Be Removed," webpage, December 23, 2016. As of September 14, 2019:
https://twitter.com/metpoliceuk/status/812298779164573696

Metz, Rachel, "Why Microsoft Accidentally Unleashed a Neo-Nazi Sexbot," *MIT Technology Review*, November 21, 2016. As of May 22, 2017:
https://www.technologyreview.com/s/601111/why-microsoft-accidentally
-unleashed-a-neo-nazi-sexbot/

Microsoft, "Bot Framework FAQ," webpage, February 20, 2019. As of September 14, 2019:
https://docs.microsoft.com/en-us/azure/bot-service/bot-service-resources-bot
-framework-faq?view=azure-bot-service-4.0

Microsoft Azure, "Language Understanding (LUIS)," webpage, undated. As of September 14, 2019:
https://www.luis.ai/

Miller, Zeke, "Romney Campaign: We Don't Buy Twitter Followers," *BuzzFeed*, July 21, 2012. As of May 23, 2017:
https://www.buzzfeed.com/zekejmiller/romney-campaign-we-dont-buy-twitter
-followers

Morris, Robert, Stephen Schueller, and Rosalind Picard, "Efficacy of a Web-Based, Crowdsourced Peer-to-Peer Cognitive Reappraisal Platform for Depression: Randomized Controlled Trial," *Journal of Medical Internet Research*, Vol. 17, No. 3, March 2015. As of April 6, 2017:
https://www.ncbi.nlm.nih.gov/pmc/articles/PMC4395771/

Munger, Kevin. "Tweetment Effects on the Tweeted: Experimentally Reducing Racist Harassment," *Political Behavior*, Vol. 39, No. 3, September 2017, pp. 629–649. As of September 14, 2019:
https://link.springer.com/article/10.1007/s11109-016-9373-5

National Police Chiefs' Council, "The Counter Terrorism Internet Referral Unit," website, undated.

NetSySLab and LERSSE, "Cyber Threats," webpage, June 17, 2016. As of April 7, 2017:
http://netsyslab.ece.ubc.ca/wiki/index.php/Cyber_Threats

OECD—*See* Organisation for Economic Co-operation and Development.

Office of the President of the United States, *International Strategy for Cyberspace: Prosperity, Security, and Openness*, Washington, D.C., May 2011. As of June 29, 2017:
https://obamawhitehouse.archives.gov/sites/default/files/rss_viewer/international_strategy_for_cyberspace.pdf

Ohlheiser, Abby, "Trolls Turned Tay, Microsoft's Fun Millennial AI Bot, into a Genocidal Maniac," *Washington Post*, March 25, 2016. As of September 18, 2020:
https://www.washingtonpost.com/news/the-intersect/wp/2016/03/24/the-internet-turned-tay-microsofts-fun-millennial-ai-bot-into-a-genocidal-maniac/

Orcutt, Mike, "Twitter Mischief Plagues Mexico's Election," *MIT Technology Review*, June 21, 2012. As of September 18, 2020:
https://www.technologyreview.com/2012/06/21/185262/twitter-mischief-plagues-mexicos-election/

Oremus, Will, "Mitt Romney's Fake Twitter Follower Problem," *Slate*, July 25, 2012. As of May 23, 2017:
http://www.slate.com/blogs/future_tense/2012/07/25/mitt_romney_fake_twitter_followers_who_s_buying_them_.html

Organisation for Economic Co-operation and Development, *OECD Guidelines for the Security of Information Systems, 1992*, Paris, France: OECD, 2002. As of May 23, 2017:
http://www.oecd.org/sti/ieconomy/oecdguidelinesforthesecurityofinformationsystems1992.htm

Paul, Christopher, and Miriam Matthews, *The Russian "Firehose of Falsehood" Propaganda Model: Why It Might Work and Options to Counter It*, Santa Monica, Calif.: RAND Corporation, PE-198-OSD, 2016. As of August 23, 2017:
https://www.rand.org/pubs/perspectives/PE198.html

Porup, J. M., "How Mexican Twitter Bots Shut Down Dissent," *Motherboard*, August 24, 2015. As of September 14, 2019:
https://www.vice.com/en_us/article/z4maww/how-mexican-twitter-bots-shut-down-dissent

Power, Mike, "What Happens When a Software Bot Goes on a Darknet Shopping Spree?" *Guardian*, December 5, 2014. As of August 23, 2017:
https://www.theguardian.com/technology/2014/dec/05/software-bot-darknet-shopping-spree-random-shopper

Public Law 112–239, National Defense Authorization Act for Fiscal Year 2013, January 2, 2013. As of May 23, 2017:
https://www.congress.gov/bill/112th-congress/house-bill/4310/text

Python Software Foundation, "fbchat 0.9.0: Facebook Chat (Messenger) for Python," webpage, November 21, 2016.

Ratkiewicz, Jacob, Michael Conover, Mark Meiss, Bruno Gonçalves, Snehal Patil, Alessandro Flammini, and Filippo Menczer, "Truthy: Mapping the Spread of Astroturf in Microblog Streams," *Proceedings of the 20th International Conference Companion on World Wide Web*, New York: Association for Computing Machinery, 2011. As of May 22, 2017:
http://dl.acm.org/citation.cfm?id=1963301

Reddit, "Reddit Content Policy," webpage, undated. As of May 23, 2017:
https://www.reddit.com/help/contentpolicy/

Regalado, Antonio, "The Biggest Technology Failures of 2016," *MIT Technology Review*, December 27, 2016. As of May 23, 2017:
https://www.technologyreview.com/s/603194/the-biggest-technology-failures-of-2016/?set=602944

Reno v. ACLU, 96 U.S. 511 (1997). As of May 23, 2017:
https://www.law.cornell.edu/supremecourt/text/521/844

Riesbeck, Christopher, and Roger Schank, *Inside Case-Based Reasoning*, Hillsdale, N.J.: L. Erlbaum Associates, 1989.

Ritter, Alan, Colin Cherry, and William Dolan, "Data-Driven Response Generation in Social Media," *Proceedings of the Conference on Empirical Methods in Natural Language Processing*, Stroudsburg, Pa.: Association for Computational Linguistics, July 2011. As of May 22, 2017:
http://dl.acm.org/citation.cfm?id=2145500

Robertson, Jordan, Michael Riley, and Andrew Willis. "How to Hack an Election," *Bloomberg Businessweek*, March 31, 2016. As of May 23, 2017:
http://www.bloomberg.com/features/2016-how-to-hack-an-election

Savage, Saiph, Andres Monroy-Hernandez, and Tobias Hollerer, "Botivist: Calling Volunteers to Action Using Online Bots," *Proceedings of the 19th ACM Conference on Computer-Supported Cooperative Work and Social Computing*, New York: Association for Computing Machinery, March 2016, pp. 813–822. As of May 22, 2017:
http://dl.acm.org/citation.cfm?id=2819985

Smith, Dave, "IBM's Watson Gets a 'Swear Filter' After Learning the Urban Dictionary," *International Business Times*, January 10, 2013. As of May 23, 2017:
http://www.ibtimes.com/ibms-watson-gets-swear-filter-after-learning-urban-dictionary-1007734

Sordoni, Alessandro, Michel Galley, Michael Auli, Chris Brockett, Yangfeng Ji, Margaret Mitchell, Jian-Yun Nie, Jianfeng Gao, and Bill Dolan, "A Neural Network Approach to Context-Sensitive Generation of Conversational Responses," *Proceedings of the North American Chapter of the Association for Computational Linguistics: Human Language Technologies*, Denver, Colo., June 22, 2015, pp. 196–205. As of May 22, 2017:
https://arxiv.org/abs/1506.06714

Stinson, Liz, "New Social Network Koko Wants to Help You Deal with Stress," *Wired*, December 16, 2015. As of May 22, 2017:
https://www.wired.com/2015/12/a-new-social-media-network-to-help-you-deal-with-stress/

Suárez-Serrato, Pablo, Margaret Roberts, Clayton Davis, and Filippo Menczer, "On the Influence of Social Bots in Online Protests," *Proceedings of the 8th International Conference on Social Informatics, Part II, LNCS*, Vol. 10047, 2016. As of May 23, 2017:
https://arxiv.org/abs/1609.08239

Subrahmanian, V. S., Amos Azaria, Skylar Durst, Vadim Kagan, Aram Galstyan, Kristina Lerman, Linhong Zhu, Emilio Ferrara, Alessandro Flammini, Fillippo Menczer, Andrew Stevens, Alexander Dekhtyar, Shuyang Gao, Tad Hogg, Farshad Kooti, Yan Liu, Onur Varol, Prashant Shiralkar, Vinod Vydiswaran, Qiaozhu Mei, and Tim Hwang, "The DARPA Twitter Bot Challenge," *Computer*, Vol. 49, No. 6, June 2016. As of September 14, 2019:
https://arxiv.org/abs/1601.05140

Suwajanakorn, Supasorn, Steven Seitz, and Ira Kemelmacher-Shlizerman, "Synthesizing Obama: Learning Lip Sync from Audio," *ACM Transactions on Graphics*, Vol. 36, No. 4, July 2017. As of August 23, 2017:
https://grail.cs.washington.edu/projects/AudioToObama/siggraph17_obama.pdf

Telegram, "Bots: An Introduction for Developers," webpage, undated. As of May 23, 2017:
https://core.telegram.org/bots

Thomas, Kurt, Chris Grier, and Vern Paxson, "Adapting Social Spam Infrastructure for Political Censorship," *Proceedings of the 5th USENIX Workshop on Large-Scale Exploits and Emergent Threats*, Berkeley, Calif.: USENIX Association, 2012. As of May 22, 2017:
http://www.icir.org/vern/papers/kremlin-bots.leet11.pdf

Torres, Gabriela, Charlotte McDonald, and Anne-Marke Tomchak, "#BBCTrending: 'I Am Tired': The Politics of Mexico's #Yamecanse Hashtag," BBC, December 9, 2014. As of May 23, 2017:
http://www.bbc.com/news/blogs-trending-30294010

Twitter, "Twitter Libraries," webpage, undated-a. As of May 22, 2017:
https://dev.twitter.com/overview/api/twitter-libraries

———, "The Twitter Rules," Twitter Help Center, undated-b. As of May 23, 2017:
https://support.twitter.com/articles/18311

———, "Automation Rules," Twitter Help Center, April 6, 2017. As of May 23, 2017:
https://support.twitter.com/articles/76915

———, "Twitter Developer Documentation," webpage, May 8, 2017. As of May 22, 2017:
https://dev.twitter.com/overview/documentation

Tyagi, Amit Kumar, and G. Aghila, "A Wide Scale Survey on Botnet," *International Journal of Computer Applications*, Vol. 34, No. 9, 2011, pp. 9–22. As of May 22, 2017:
http://citeseerx.ist.psu.edu/viewdoc/download?doi=10.1.1.259.5081&rep=rep1&type=pdf

United Nations, International Covenant on Civil and Political Rights, New York, December 16, 1966. As of May 23, 2017:
http://www.ohchr.org/EN/ProfessionalInterest/Pages/CCPR.aspx

U.S. Code Title 18, Section 2339A, Providing Material Support to Terrorists, November 2, 2002. As of May 23, 2017:
https://www.law.cornell.edu/uscode/text/18/2339A

U.S. Code Title 22, Section 1431, United States Information and Educational Exchange Act of 1948 (Smith-Mundt Act), January 27, 1948. As of September 14, 2019:
https://www.law.cornell.edu/uscode/text/22/chapter-18

U.S. Code, Title 44, Section 3541, Federal Information Security Management Act of 2002, December 17, 2002. As of May 23, 2017:
http://csrc.nist.gov/drivers/documents/FISMA-final.pdf

U.S. Department of Defense, *Law of War Manual*, Washington, D.C.: Office of General Counsel Department of Defense, June 12, 2015. As of May 23, 2017:
http://archive.defense.gov/pubs/Law-of-War-Manual-June-2015.pdf

Vincent, James, "Twitter Taught Microsoft's AI Chatbot to Be a Racist Asshole in Less Than a Day," *Verge*, March 24, 2016. As of May 23, 2017:
http://www.theverge.com/2016/3/24/11297050/tay-microsoft-chatbot-racist

———, "Baidu Launches Medical Chatbot to Help Chinese Doctors Diagnose Patients," The *Verge*, October 11, 2016. As of May 22, 2017:
http://www.theverge.com/2016/10/11/13240434/baidu-medical-chatbot-china-melody

Volkert, Zachary, "Mexican President Enrique Peña Nieto Paid $600,000 to Rig Elections with Hacking and Fake Social Media Profiles, Alleges Jailed Hacker," *Inquisitr*, April 1, 2016. As of May 23, 2017:
http://www.inquisitr.com/2949327/mexican-president-enrique-pena-nieto-paid-600000-to-rig-elections-with-hacking-and-fake-social-media-profiles-alleges-jailed-hacker/

Warrick, Joby, "How a U.S. Team Uses Facebook, Guerilla Marketing to Peel Off Potential ISIS Recruits," *Washington Post*, February 6, 2017. As of May 23, 2017: https://www.washingtonpost.com/world/national-security/bait-and-flip-U.S.-team-uses-facebook-guerrilla-marketing-to-peel-off-potential-isis-recruits/2017/02/03/431e19ba-e4e4-11e6-a547-5fb9411d332c_story.html?utm_term=.b408c0c5819d

Watts, Clint, "Disinformation: A Primer in Russian Active Measures and Influence Campaigns," statement prepared for a U.S. Senate Select Committee on Intelligence Hearing, Washington, D.C., March 30, 2017. As of August 23, 2017: https://www.intelligence.senate.gov/sites/default/files/documents/os-cwatts-033017.pdf

Weisburd, Andrew, Clint Watts, and J. M. Berger, "Trolling for Trump: How Russia Is Trying to Destroy Our Democracy," *War on the Rocks*, November 6, 2016. As of May 22, 2017:
https://warontherocks.com/2016/11/trolling-for-trump-how-russia-is-trying-to-destroy-our-democracy/

Wisniewski, Mary, "How Bots Can Connect Banks and Millennials," *American Banker*, August 1, 2016. As of May 16, 2017:
https://www.americanbanker.com/news/how-bots-can-connect-banks-and-millennials

Woolley, Samuel, "Automating Power: Social Bot Interference in Global Politics," *First Monday*, Vol. 21, No. 4, 2016. As of May 22, 2017:
http://firstmonday.org/ojs/index.php/fm/rt/printerFriendly/6161/5300

Woolley, Samuel, and Douglas Guilbeault, *Computational Propaganda in the United States of America: Manufacturing Consensus Online*, Oxford, UK: University of Oxford, Working Paper No. 2017.5, May 2017. As of August 23, 2017: http://comprop.oii.ox.ac.uk/wp-content/uploads/sites/89/2017/06/Comprop-USA.pdf

Zablocki v. Redhail, 434 U.S. 374 (1978). As of May 23, 2017:
https://www.oyez.org/cases/1977/76-879

Zhang, Jinxue, Rui Zhang, Yanchao Zhang, and Guanhua Yan, "The Rise of Social Botnets: Attacks and Countermeasures," Cornell University arXiv:1603.02714 [cs.SI], March 8, 2016. As of May 22, 2017: https://arxiv.org/abs/1603.02714